A
Fleeting
Glimpse
at
Most

Fragments of a Memoir by Bernard Shull

Publishing Coordinator – Sharon Kizziah-Holmes

Paperback-Press
an imprint of A & S Publishing
Paperback Press, LLC

ISBN -13: 978-1-956806-82-3

DEDICATION

For Janice, Abby and Ira
also, for Mari

[FRONT PIECE]

Untitled

The things to come in future times,
The things that are already gone,
Are but a wisp of spider thread
A dream, a mist at dawn

You cannot touch them, feel them
You cannot hold them close
You can but see them in your mind
A fleeting glimpse at most

Yes, future is the things to come
And past the things that are gone
And one is made of spider thread
The other, mist a dawn

Written about the age of 11 or 12, looking from my bedroom
window across the alleyway at the rear windows and garages of the
row houses on Euclid Street

CONTENTS

INTRODUCTION

This book is not a memoir, and it's certainly not an autobiography. Many of the writings are, nevertheless, 'memiorish' or autobiographical in nature. They are, as the title suggests, 'a fleeting glimpse at most' of my life and interests as I see them.

The writing took place during my winter excursions to Florida between 2006-2019 while participating in the weekly meetings of the 'Naples Writers' Forum.' This ever-changing group was organized and lead by the incomparable Mari Messer who offered her own exceptional writings, provided encouragement to others, and always helpful commentary. Most of all, through some sort of managerial alchemy, she converted the competitive spirit of self-absorbed writers into a camaraderie that made Saturday mornings an event.

My daughter, Abby Ruth Sernoff and my son, Ira David Shull, who died in 2016 read many of the pieces below and have, through their responses and in a variety of other ways, helped me develop and prepare the material. It was Abby who discovered the lurid information that is contained in "Searching for Jake and Lyla." No one, however, has been more important and influential than Janice, my wife and companion of 60 years. With a far better temperament than me, it is beyond my understanding how she has been able to read repeated drafts, and always provide useful comments.

What's left to be said is said below.

I

WHY WRITE

To write or not to write. 'Whether 'tis nobler in the mind to suffer the slings and arrows of outrageous fortune, or to take up pen or laptop and, by writing about it....' Well, you get the idea. There may be as many reasons for writing as there are writers, but underlying all is the desire to communicate, serve a purpose, maybe, counter 'outrageous fortune.' For some, writing is "to be" rather than "not to be."

What is communicated is always informational in a broad sense, but may be a combination of fact and imagination. It may be fiction, non-fiction, creative non-fiction, science fiction, "ripped from the headlines," "based on a true story," or some garbled combination of all of these things aimed, as the modern aphorism puts it, 'to reveal a deeper truth.'

The advantage to writing over speaking, the other principal form of communication, is that in writing one can make corrections, rewrite and improve the product. John Kenneth Galbraith, who seemingly wrote with careless grace, once remarked that 'spontaneity comes after the 5th draft.'

But even with repeated revision, writing can be risky. You might still say something you later regret. There are, of course, ways to mitigate the risk. You can, at the top of your writing, place the word "DRAFT," or "WORKING PAPER," or "NOT FOR PUBLICATION," or some such notice meaning: "Don't take this seriously unless you like it." This works for books and articles and maybe for essays and short stories–even poems. But it doesn't work on e-mail or letters to friends, or on a resume to a potential employer.

Writing, moreover, whether cursive, print or digital, leaves a permanent record. You'd be surprised how much is kept indefinitely, somewhere in a desk drawer or on computer disk. A number of years ago, a large corporation came under investigation for conspiring to fix prices–a crime that could send its executives to jail. On subpoenaing the company's files, Justice Department lawyers found a letter sent to its competitors establishing the prices to be charged the following month. At the bottom of the letter was the instruction: "Burn After Reading." A conscientious secretary had saved a copy, as she did copies of all important documents.

In contrast, speaking provides relatively easy retreats. If you say something you wish you hadn't, you can 'walk it back,' saying: "I didn't really mean that; sorry if it sounded the way it did; let me make myself clear." Or you can place the onus on the listener: "You misheard, or misinterpreted what I said;" or "you've taken it out of context." You can dodge the consequences by explaining that "this is what I really meant." The spoken words evaporate into the ether, unless somehow recorded, their meaning obscured by nuance and the failure of memory.

Some just find speaking is easier. They can talk with fervor and imagination, but have great difficulty translating their thoughts into intelligible composition. They find writing to be hard work and a risky enterprise.

Hamlet may have felt that way. Hamstrung by wary contemplation, he might have ruminated on the question of whether or not to write. He spoke beautifully: "To die, to sleep. To sleep, perchance to dream—ay, there's the rub. For in that sleep of death what dreams may come when we have shuffled off this mortal coil..." To the best of my knowledge, he never put his words to paper. We are fortunate that somebody else came along who did.

II

LOOKING BACK AT THINGS LONG GONE

As a child, I lived in a neighborhood in northwest Philadelphia called Wynnefield. The homes ranged from relatively inexpensive row houses to prestigious estates and near-mansions. The neighborhood was bordered by Fairmount Park, the main-line of the Pennsylvania Railroad and City Line Avenue that separated it from Bala Cynwyd, a wealthy main-line community in Lower Merion township.

I walked to school each day from the time I was 5 until I graduated high school at 17. In the summer, I played on the streets, in the back alleys and in what seemed to me at the time a vast wasteland through which the railroad ran; everyone called it 'The Lot.' I traveled around the area walking, on a bicycle and into the city riding on trolley cars and the subway. I was born again when I entered college at Temple University, mentored by teachers who were devoted to teaching.

Epiphany

When I was very young, a man appeared
each evening to light gas lamps on the street
Horse-drawn wagons brought milk to the back door
School rooms had inkwells and window poles
The school year went on forever,
we thought summer would too

In summer, we changed from knickers to short pants
played along a railroad track with dirty hands, muddy shoes,
bruised knees, watched trains plunge into the unknown,
Prickly 'stickers' from bull thistle plants clung to our clothes.
we pulled clumps of grass-held soil from the ground
to throw at friends and passing cars

On Sunday in the park, I walked a dirt path through
brushwood and shrubs, under the arching bows of leafy
trees, into a hidden clearing. Stung by silence,
I asked, of no one in particular, is all of this for me?
The response was only drops of water,
dripping from a tree

returning to gather in rivers, streams and clouds
to come again in rain and mist, or splash some
rocky beach with foam and spray, adrift in
spider webs of chance, spinning behind,
from whispers of my childhood
in the forest of my mind

The Lot

I was seven years old when I first saw it at the end of the block where I lived. Bordered by a well-traveled street appropriately called Upland Way, it was a very wide, and long three-story deep depression that stretched out as far as I could see–an urban canyon with a dirt floor that was mostly level and rock-hard. The mainline of the old Pennsylvania Railroad, running from Philadelphia to Chicago, occupied its far edge. We knew it as 'The Lot.'

Semi-pro baseball teams played there in the early summer evenings, with the players wearing jerseys advertising local businesses. Boys around my age and a little older would go there to run, play and just horse around. There were easy ways to get to the bottom, but we favored sliding down its cliff-like side; or running through a weed-infested path on a rocky protrusion that wound circuitously to its floor.

For us, the lot became a focal point, particularly in the summer when school was out, a place to run, jump and in general exhaust ourselves. It became a reference in conversation:

Where do you live? About a block from the lot.

Where do you go to school? Not far from the lot.

In football games on the street, the play caller might say, "Joey, run five steps toward the lot and turn left."

To get to high school, we would walk over the canyon-like depression on a bridge, back and forth each day. The first day I crossed the bridge, I saw a dead body hanging from the back of a billboard on the rim of the lot. A hobo who had been riding the rails? I never knew. My last vivid memory of the lot was looking at it from the window of a high school classroom, watching a long freight train traveling west and counting its cars in Spanish.

By that time, the lot was just another familiar place, a silent presence that had once served a purpose. It wasn't until much later, long after I had left the area, that I began to think about it as something else. That hole in the ground had been a playing field, a stage for dramatic performance; its railroad was a magic carpet that brought to mind strange places and distant people; it was a loadstar and a launching pad for what was to come next, stirring imagination shaping expectations. For us, it was a little like *The Frontier* that some historians believed forged the American character; or *The Moor* in *The Hound of the Baskervilles* that exerted a menacing influence on those who lived there. In my local area, we grew up under the influence of *The Lot*.

I don't believe it could exist today. For one thing, whoever owned it would know it was an 'attractive nuisance' and fence it off to keep the kids out. Passing through the old neighborhood some years ago, I found that, in fact, it doesn't exist anymore. A national bakery had constructed a multi-building facility in its depths. Workers drove down to the buildings on a steeply graded road. Trucks moved back and forth from street level. Tall brick chimneys emitted billowing white clouds that permeated the area with the smell of warm bread. The magical canyon with a railroad running through it that I first saw at the age of seven had, like 'all good customs yielded to the new.' It had disappeared in a puff of smoke.

An Afternoon in the Park

On a warm Sunday summer morning, with the war in Europe and the Pacific still raging, three of us, about 13 years old, hiked down a long cobblestoned hill toward Fairmount Park, a vast expanse of wooded grassland that redeems the crowded city streets of Philadelphia. On the edge of the park, we boarded an 'open trolley,' no doors or windows, tied to an electrical wire above by a connecting rod on its roof. The trolley traveled along a narrow track, through the grassy fields, under overhanging branches, around curves hidden by thick clumps of shrubs, open to the sights and smells of the park.

We jumped on board, with our brown bags filled with bologna, cheese and egg salad sandwiches, holding on to the poles along the sides of the open trolley, faces to the air that rushed by as it chugged its way across the Schuylkill river, finally coming to a stop in Strawberry Mansion – a commercial neighborhood with rundown houses that hadn't seen a strawberry plant for a hundred years and had no mansions that we ever noticed.

Leaving the trolley, we walked through the still-quiet Sunday-morning streets, joking, complaining, bumping along, and looking at the few people who were about in this 'foreign' neighborhood. After about 20 minutes of walking, we saw the large, multi-storied building without a roof – a block-wide, a block-long with huge light stanchions projecting from its walls and surrounded by parked cars.

Paying 25 cents, we walked through the turnstiles into the dark cavern of Connie Mack Stadium (née Shibe Park) with its dirty floors and rich aroma of food, abandoned newspapers, and unidentifiable debris left by long-departed crowds. We ran up the dimly lit, concrete steps, and into the stands. There it was, the glistening green sea of low-cut grass, broken by dirt paths connecting white bases, a pitcher's mound with its corridor leading to the batter's box, and white lines defining what was fair and foul. We stood for a moment in wonder at the sight; and then rushed to find our seats, avoiding the stanchions holding the upper deck that cut off vision. We watched as the players took batting practice and the pitchers threw warm-up tosses. We talked, and shouted as the grounds crew smoothed out the dirt and repainted the lines with chalk. Game time approached and the stands filled for the Sunday 'double-header.'

The players emerged from somewhere within the bowels of the stadium, striding into the dugout and onto the field. In their white and grey uniforms, they stood, hats in hand, as the national anthem was played. We also stood, and cheered as the anthem finished with the familiar words, "...play ball."

There was Schoolboy Roe, an old-timer now, and Dutch Leonard, with his mysterious knuckle ball, Willie Puddin' Head Jones, reputed to be a little slow, and Granny Hamner, young at 18 or 19. Also, Harry "the Hat," Whitey, Andy, Dell, Robin, and a bunch of others. We watched while they pitched, hit the ball, fielded grounders, converted double plays and swatted foul balls. We cheered when they sliced hard liners that curved, as if on an invisible track, over third base toward the left field wall; and when they smacked ground balls that hopped in unimaginable ways, or drove long flies against the formidable right field wall–high enough to keep people in the upper stories of the buildings across the street from selling tickets to their windows. We talked, calculated batting averages in our head and team standings if we won or lost. We guessed what was going to happen, and second guessed when it didn't.

The innings rolled on, the sun moving across the sky and shadows creeping out of the batters' box toward the pitchers' mound. Five hours of baseball on a slow summer afternoon, watching the game unfold on a green pasture, dirt paths with dusty white bases, munching on bologna, cheese and egg salad sandwiches.

Memorial Hall Memory

In the neighborhood where I grew up, basketball was the after-school game of choice. We played in schoolyards where the backboard was flush against a brick wall, and strong moves to the basket were bone-breaking hazards. We nailed backboards to telephone poles and to our own poles dug into back alleys. We played in the rain, we played in the snow, clearing off our 'court,' and at night with the ground illuminated by lights shining in kitchen windows.

On occasion, we would find an inside arena. Philadelphia's Memorial Hall in Fairmount Park was one of these. With marble floors, granite walls, an immensely high ceiling over its central vestibule, it was capped by an iron and glass dome. The building had been a focal point for the nation's Centennial Exposition of 1876 where it exhibited art sent from all over the world. It remained the city's art gallery until the current Art Museum opened in 1928–the 'Greek Temple' with the iconic 72 steps that Sylvester Stalone ascended in the movie "Rocky." Once the new Art Museum opened, Memorial Hall became little more than a vacant reminder of an historic celebration. Sometime in the late 1940s, the Fairmount Park Commission turned the building into a recreation center. The central hall was ideal for basketball, if you didn't mind playing on a stone floor. At 15 and 16, neither I nor my friends gave it a thought.

So we played. I came flying from the corner, sliding through the outstretched arms of opponents, legs pumping, mind racing...one-one thousand, two-one thousand, three...and the ball arrived in my hands. Without hesitation, I rose easily into the air, saw the basket twenty feet away, and let it go. The ball arched high, reached its peak and curved down through the net without touching the rim. I didn't actually see the ball go through the basket, but I didn't have to. I *knew* it did. You can know such things when you're moving in rhythm with the flow of the game.

I didn't see the ball pass through the net because, as I came down, I slipped, fell to the floor and hit my head. In a daze, I felt myself lifted and carried somewhere by people I didn't recognize. I came to my senses as they placed me in a car that took me to the emergency room of a nearby hospital. A doctor felt a bump growing on my head, looked in my eyes and patched a cut on my chin. Without an X-ray, MRI, or CAT scan, he pronounced me fit. He asked if I wanted to stay for a while. I said no and left with friends.

I hadn't thought about Memorial Hall for years. The experience returned in a waking dream after a discussion a few days earlier with a high school classmate who I hadn't seen for a very long time. Remembering my 20 foot shot reawakened a feeling of pure bliss. It wasn't because the shot was successful. It was the memory of the moment. The normal dissonance of conflicting demands and uncertainty had given way to illumination, confidence in a clear course of action and knowledge of its certain outcome. In the middle of physical engagement and mental distraction, I knew that the ball couldn't do anything but go through the hoop, even as I came back to earth and bumped my head on the marble floor of that grand old building. Such surges of comprehension don't occur all that often. They are worth remembering, even one that was nothing more than a long-ago jump-shot in a forgotten game of pick-up basketball.

On South Mountain

In my early 'getting-an-education years,' I had a number of summer jobs. I worked as an assistant director of a recreation center, a file clerk in the office of a whiskey distiller, a Good Humor man selling ice cream from a truck, and a door-to-door salesman of cemetery plots. But of all the jobs that occupied my summers, none had the lasting impact of working as a waiter at an run-down resort hotel called South Mountain Manor that was located in the Appalachian highlands, west of the Lehigh Valley.

My friend Allan found the job at the hotel, and asked if I would be interested. I was completing my freshman year in college when I met with the owner in his cluttered office in Philadelphia–a gruff, weather-beaten old-timer in a worn-out sport jacket. He somehow got the impression that I had experience. "How hard can it be," I asked myself?"

Allan and I, along with other waiters arrived in late May, a week or so before the hotel opened for the season. The main facility was a rectangular building, several stories high, with a large dining room, a kitchen, auditorium, and an expansive porch overlooking the surrounding property. It was in decent condition compared to the six or seven shabby clapboard guest houses that dotted the surrounding grounds. "Rustic," was the owner's description. "They have to be fixed-up before the guests arrive."

He intended the waiters to be the 'fixer-uppers.' They were given jobs that included some lifting, hauling, cleaning and painting. Armed with a watery white paint, Allan and I were told to paint the mahogany paneled walls in a bedroom of one of the houses. "You can see the brown through the white," Allan complained as he brushed. The paint dripped on our clothes, shoes, faces, hands and floor. We decided we might as well paint the floor. With the door blocked by wet paint, we escaped through a window. No one ever asked us to paint again.

The guests, typically families with children, were booked for a week or two. Whatever had been accomplished to improve their living quarters, and it wasn't much, they seemed happy enough during the warm days, cool evenings, and nightly entertainment in the dining hall.

The 'help,' on the other hand, found the management laughable. How could the owner have expected the waiters to repair the guest houses? It also became clear that the tips, on which we relied, would not be much. Whether from disappointment or youthful exuberance, a spontaneously dysfunctional labor-management relationship developed. On the labor side it took the form of loud parties after work, drunken escapades, breaking the rules that kept the male and female staff apart at night, a walk-out protest of the 'second chef' who cooked inedible breakfasts for the waiters, and a general attitude of disrespect for authority. The management for its part resorted to covert observation, surprise raids on non-permitted activities and empty threats.

All this was great fun for someone just turned 19. Through it all, I even learned to be a waiter. Among other things, I mastered the notable feat of carrying a large metal tray loaded with heavy dishes with one hand above my head, while opening the door from the kitchen to the dining room and conveying the dinner plates to the appropriate tables.

What was truly unforgettable about the summer, however, were the people. Albert, the good-natured head chef, had learned his trade in the dining cars of the Pennsylvania Railroad. The kitchen staff sang songs with a beat that I later learned was rock-and-roll. Harry 'Lifty' Lewis, the resident stand-up comic, earned his nickname by stealing his jokes from others. His blond wife, who we called 'Queenie,' was rumored to have been in burlesque. The young women counselors who cared for the children were our sirens: Naomi, a barefoot flower-child before there were flower children; Phyllis, too young to be working here, but grown beyond her years. And Goldie, a self-confident, penetrating intelligence, interested in and loved by everyone. Finally the struggling owner. "Keep the water glasses full," he ordered the waiters, "so the guests won't eat so much."

The summer passed through routine days and bizarre nights. When it was over, I emerged with hardly any earnings, but with a new belief in my ability to cope with the absurd. I wondered if there would ever be a summer like it again. There wasn't.

Over the years, I maintained a friendship with many of those waiters and counselors I met at South Mountain, and heard about others. They became lawyers and musicians, dentists, and teachers. One became a marine and then an actuary. None that I know of ended up in jail. Several marriages resulted from the night-time liaisons, and later a few divorces.

The hotel is gone now. And so are most of the people who were there, including Allan. Soon, there will be no one who remembers, and the hotel will truly disappear. But the South Mountain, itself, endures. The breeze that cooled families fleeing the hot city still whispers across the upland meadow. I like to think that if I returned and listened carefully, I might still hear the sounds of the old hotel, the shouts of the children in the pool, the laughter of the guests at the nightly shows, and maybe even the echoes of my joy at everything that was new.

Butterfly Memories

Winds to blow, shapes to touch
Wings uncurl in flight
Through unending grassy plains
Flutter, dart, alight

Floating through the waves of time,
Beyond the shaded past
Heading for what's meant to be
Weaving in the moving air

Rushing toward the light and dark
The past a dream arising
of lying in a silken home
metamorphasizing

Selling Ice Cream

Up in the morning about 8:00 am, I put on my white shirt and pants, had breakfast and ran out of the house carrying a black clip-on bow-tie and a Sam Browne belt. A bus got me to the yard about 10:30. It was going to be hot today, a good day to sell ice cream.

I had just completed my sophomore year in college, and had found a job driving an ice-cream truck, down city streets, ringing a bell, alerting the neighborhood that the ice cream man was here. The truck was white, with Good Humor Ice Cream in large black letters on the side, and a picture of a chocolate bar. It had a large block-like ice-cream compartment in the back, accessible through side and rear hatches, that sealed in the cold, and an open driver compartment in front that could be covered by a canvass top, in case of rain. The engine, as I recall, had a governor that would not allow the truck to reach a speed of more than 40 miles an hour, making drag racing pretty much impossible.

When I got to my truck in the morning, I loaded it with enough dry ice to keep the ice cream frozen during the day and evening. I then filled it with Good Humor ice cream bars, creamsicles, cones, sandwiches and cups. My favorite was the "Toasted Almond" bar, but the Orange Creamsicle was pretty good too. I didn't eat much. The pay was a percentage of the net sales revenue you came back with each day. You were not charged for unsold product that was returned. Driving a truck, I had to join the Teamster's Union. I never met Jimmy Hoffa and I don't know what happened to him.

I would start out around 11:30 for the residential neighborhoods of southwest Philadelphia and my convoluted route. My selling day began just after lunch. I slowly drove by long lines of row houses on streets filled with kids out of school for the summer, playing on sidewalks and in the street. I would ring my bell, stop from time-to-time and wait for customers to congregate. Getting out of the truck, I would turn to those in line, taking the ice cream they wanted from the cardboard boxes inside the cold compartment. A baseball game on an empty lot, or anywhere a crowd had gathered was a good place to stop, one eye on the people lining up, one eye on the back of the truck; occasionally someone would open the unlocked back hatch and reach for the bars and cones.

So the day and evening went, driving and selling through dinner time, with kids alerted by the bell, running down the street after the truck, a virtual pied piper, with mothers running after their children, yelling for them to wait for 'Jack & Jill,' they're cheaper. But, I murmured, their ice cream is not as good.

About 7:00-7:30, I headed back to the yard, sometimes under threatening skies, hoping the rain would hold off, because the canvass roof allowed it to come in from the side. I cashed out for the day and headed home, arriving around 9:30 pm, tired enough to go to sleep; waking up the next day to do it again.

That summer I learned how to drive in the city, get out of tight spaces and negotiate the open road to my route at 40 miles-an-hour. I brought delight to children and sometimes despair to their mothers; but normally felt the welcoming wave of 'the ice cream man is here' as I drove through.

It's been a long time since I thought of ice cream as a magical treat that gave relief from steamy city sidewalks, before anyone had air conditioning, and families sat outside on their stoops in the early evening to get some air. Ever since, whenever I hear an ice cream truck, playing a song or ringing its bell, moving slowly down the street, I look up and say to myself, "I know you, I know what you're doing, I even know what you're thinking. I'll have a 'Chocolate Eclair Bar' or maybe a 'Toasted Almond.'

Around Every Bend in the Road

Just passed my 21st birthday, I was leaving my home in Philadelphia, perhaps for good, going to graduate school and a teaching assistantship in Economics at the University of Illinois. But before that, in mid-August, I was driving to California, the land of my fantasies, with a friend who owned a pre-World War II Ford. The first day out, we moved smoothly across the Pennsylvania Turnpike, struggled through the congestion of Pittsburgh and crossed the Ohio River into West Virginia.

It was my turn to drive as we reached the highlands of West Virginia on a rainy Friday evening. The rain had begun to sweep across the windshield; drops banged on the hood and roof, making the narrow, two-lane road slippery. I reached the top of a steep hill. Below lay the city of Weirton and the National Steel Company. Looking ahead, I was mesmerized by the blast furnaces in the valley that spasmodically erupted, shooting yellow-orange pillars of flame into the cloud-blackened sky.

Descending and distracted, the tires squealed as the road turned and the car skidded to the left. I regained control and straightened out on the wrong side. I turned the wheel, but not fast enough to avoid side-swiping a car driving up the hill. "Damn," I thought, "but no one hurt, no real damage." It was my last composed thought for some time. I had side-swiped a police cruiser. The insult *majeure,* it turned out, was that the collision had eradicated the official department insignia from the side of the car.

Two officers got out of the cruiser, looked at us, then at the damage. "Okay, boys," said one, "get out of the car." They escorted us to the cruiser. Turning to his partner, the lead officer told him to "call the station, and have them set up the gallows in back." He also managed to alert a tow-truck to tow our car to a garage.

We got to the station after midnight and were placed in a holding cell. After a while, a young woman came by, told us she was a local reporter and asked what had happened. She came back later, looked in on us and called: "Have a nice weekend, guys." An officer said we would be held for a judge the next morning. We didn't think they would hang us.

We stayed that night in the cell, sleeping on wooden benches. When Saturday morning arrived, we waited for the judge, and waited...and then waited some more. He didn't arrive until mid-afternoon. It had rained through the night, threatening to flood the steel mill, and he had been stacking sandbags. Finally, the judge ascended the bench, determined that our insurance would pay to repair the damage to the cruiser, levied a fine and released us to reclaim our car. At the garage we were told our steering was defective. We paid a bill for a repair to the steering, and left as quickly as possible.

The fine and the cost of the car repair had depleted my savings. I decided it would be cheaper to hitch-hike and camp out than continue with my friend who was determined to stay in motels and eat at restaurants. Somewhere near Jefferson City, Missouri, suitcase in hand and duffle bag on my shoulder, I began to hike along Route 54.

In Kansas, far from any city lights, I found little traffic, but a night sky filled with stars I had never seen before. Along the western strip of Oklahoma, I caught a ride with a Texas rancher who offered me a job. I thanked him and moved on. I crossed the northern edge of the Texas panhandle and landed in Tucumcari, New Mexico. There I found a run-down hotel where the lobby was populated by cowboys and cicadas. Next morning, a taxi driver stopped to offer me a ride to the highway. I told him I had no money, but he said, "get in" and gave me a lift to Route 66. There, I hitched to Albuquerque. Standing on the roadside, two military policemen pulled up in a jeep to ask for identification and my draft card. Satisfied I was not a deserter, they left in time for me to find a ride with a semi-pro baseball player traveling to California with his young son, going home after his season had ended in Minnesota. He was tired and asked me to do some of the driving. In return for driving his new "Olds 88," he paid for my hotel room in Flagstaff. Without incident, we crossed the mountains and desert to Needles, Barstow and into Los Angles.

When I got to my relatives, they didn't have a bed to spare. I slept on the floor. No matter! Except for the smog that burned my eyes every morning, I could not have felt better. I had seen blast furnaces light-up the night sky, spent a night in a jail cell, camped under a star-lit heaven, met cowboys and cicadas, been braced by military police and helped-out by a taxi-driver, a Texas rancher and a baseball player. Released by a West Virginia judge, I had been released again, traveling through a new and strange world, buoyed by good fortune, the kindness of strangers and a marvel around every bend in the road.

III

FINDING A CAREER

After reading Lincoln Steffens's Autobiography in Junior High School, I decided I wanted to be a 'muck-raking' reporter. The closest I came was sports editor of my high school newspaper. Taking up economics as profession came later, the result of a more convoluted passage.

Three Recollections: Looking Back at Starting-Up

Talking

On a grassy, freshman campus
called Cedarbrook, in a Philadelphia suburb,
World War II-style wooden barracks dot the landscape
and serve as classrooms and student union.
New college students gather to try-out
for freshman debate.
They stand, one-by-one, giving two-minute
talks on their chosen subjects. I rise
my first ever public address:
"Good afternoon"
I have no subject to speak of, murmur
a few words and stand silent,
A blood-red curtain descends hiding the
audience I say, "Thank you,"
sit down
Brevity being elegant, and in short supply for this group
I'm invited to join the team

Walking

August morning, hot and dusty
New Mexico, Tucumcari,
Route 54 meets 66
cowboys lounge, cicadas sing
Duffle bag and battered suitcase
Taxi stops:
"To the highway?"
"Can't pay"
"That's OK"
Take a cab to thumb a ride
to Albuquerque, then LA
sweat dripping, blacktop waving,
walking on a Summer day

Waking

Restored by sleep, I lay
on a narrow bed in my rented room
eyes wide open, late for class
'year at Spring 'day at morn,'
sun shines through the window glass,
over a rolling prairie
of newly planted corn
'larks on the wing'
I hear birds sing
the grass 'dew pearled'
reviving the world
'Gods in his heaven'
I'm in Illinois

Ed Young's Passing Stirred Memories

I was saddened when I received an e-mail from an old friend who told me that Ed Young, former Chancellor of the University of Wisconsin, had died. When I arrived in Madison in 1954, Young had been Chairman of the Economics Department. I found him to be a shrewd, hard-headed administrator who 'planned ahead.' His passing stirred a distant memory of my time at the University and, for reasons not completely clear, a memory of an even earlier time.

The message initially brought to mind a warm, sunny day on Lake Mendota. After a long, brutally cold winter, the ice and snow were gone, the grass and trees alive, the water sparkling with bits of sunshine, reflecting off the foliage that surrounded it. I spotted a diving board, and the water looked inviting. I hadn't dived in years, but on that day in Madison, I thought I would give it a try. Diving, it turned out, was not like riding a bicycle, at least not for me. I found I couldn't perform the front flips and back dives I had learned at a young age. I invariably ended flopping on my side or back. After more than a few tries, I gave up, deciding I'd just as soon avoid any further damage to body and pride.

Resigned to the disappointment of departed muscle memory, my thoughts turned to earlier days when, at 12 or 13, I had learned how to dive on Mirror Lake in Browns Mills, New Jersey. The diving platform there was anchored in the deep brownish water, colored by tannins from decaying roots of the surrounding pine trees. I watched some of the older teenagers spring from the board into the air, curving their bodies to the side so that they entered the water at an oblique angle. I asked my cousin Les what they called that. He said, what else, it was a 'side-dive.'

"How," I asked, "do they do it?"

"Wherever they turn their heads," he explained, "their bodies follow." I tried. It worked. I had learned the secret of diving.

That summer, applying the principle, I was able to do the 'side dive;' and also a back flip and a front flip, somersaulting in the air with my legs tucked close to my body, and landing in the water feet first. I also learned the back dive. Toes on the end of the board, my back to the water, I propelled my body upward, moved my head backward and my body arching through the air until I broke the surface of the water, hands first and legs pointing straight up. The back dive was an act of faith in my prevision, my sense of invulnerability, and a conviction that no one would remove the water while I wasn't looking.

By the time I reached Madison, I had long forgotten about diving. My energies had been consumed by academic studies, and it was on these that Ed Young had an impact. I had come to Wisconsin on a fellowship. After my first year, he called me into his office, no doubt, I thought, to praise me for my excellent work. Hardly! He informed me that my fellowship would not be renewed; it was needed to attract students from outside the University. Not having any other source of income, I was both angry and distressed. But, Ed Young had an alternative that was better than a fellowship. It was a research assistantship with Professor Edwin Witte, a driving force in the Department whose class I had taken my first semester. As matters turned out, my association with Witte proved helpful the rest of the way through my graduate work. He subsequently found me another fellowship and smoothed the path for the completion of my dissertation.

It was years after I left Madison that Ed Young became Chancellor. In 1970 he achieved a sort of national fame that I know he would have happily avoided. On August 24, a bomb exploded on campus in Sterling Hall. A researcher was killed and others were injured. During my time in Madison, Sterling Hall had housed the Economics Department; all my classes had been there. The Economics Department had, however, moved. When the bomb went off, Sterling was occupied by the Physics Department. Radicals, protesting the Vietnam War, had taken exception to contracts that tied the Physics Department to the Pentagon.

Chancellor Young responded by calling in the National Guard. He said the protestors "...wanted to close the university — the one place where they were free to speak and protest....." To this day, his role in quelling the unrest has remained a sensitive topic at Wisconsin. Some defended his call for troops by saying that he insisted they not have bullets in their guns.

Ed Young's struggles at Wisconsin have faded, some of them into the history books. For me, his passing summoned an appreciation for his competence and good will. It had brought to mind a frustrating day in Madison on Lake Mendota, and then, looking back through the wrong end of a telescope to earlier time when I was 12 or 13 years old. I walked to the end of a diving board, launched myself into the air, using my head to direct my body and, after a timeless flight, plunged into the brown water of Mirror Lake in Browns Mills, from which I emerged into a future where I would happily meet Ed Young and mourn his passing.

Ed Witte's Cow-Catcher

When I first met Ed Witte in 1954, he was 67 years old, a round, bald-headed steam engine of a man who could bulldoze his way through obstacles. As a new graduate student in the Department of Economics at Wisconsin, I learned he was an important faculty member, and that he had accomplished something significant during the 1930s. I wasn't sure what it was. When the fellowship that attracted me to the University expired at the end of my first year, Witte hired me as his research assistant, paid for, I was later told, out of his own pocket.

The job was neither difficult nor time-consuming. I read articles on social security, and provided him with summaries for a manuscript he was preparing. He never commented on my summaries except to say they were fine. When the year was up, he arranged another fellowship.

As my faculty advisor, he would normally have overseen my dissertation. But I was writing on a subject outside his expertise. While he remained my advisor, he arranged for me to meet with Corwin Edwards at the University of Chicago, a nationally-known expert in the area I had chosen. I met with Edwards to discuss my proposed work. He made some helpful suggestions. And he hired me to gather information and conduct interviews for a book he was writing to be published by the Brookings Institution. His book was directly pertinent to the subject I had chosen. I could not use the interview material I obtained in my dissertation. But what I learned in the interviews and in discussion with Edwards enriched my work materially.

Ed Witte was not a conventional teacher. He was long on opinions and anecdotes, and short on rigor. Students sometimes complained. "Yes, he wrote some laws for the state government and in Washington, but that was only legislative draftsmanship." "Yes, he was a member of the War Labor Board during World War II, but that was just an administrative job."

His opinions and anecdotes, however, were enlightening. He talked from personal experience about people I had read about,

Harold Ickes, Franklin Roosevelt's Secretary of the Interior, and Harry Hopkins, his special assistant. When, at the War Labor Board in the 1940s, he resolved a labor dispute at General Motors by calling officials at DuPont, where the control resided. He lured Francis Perkins, the former Secretary of Labor and Wayne Morse, the independent Senator from Oregon, to the University for seminars.

He once told a story about growing up on a farm in Wisconsin; and coming to Madison as an impoverished student. When he needed to go to Milwaukee, with no money for a train ticket, he rode the cow-catcher. It was a long time before I figured that one out. A couple of years ago, looking at pictures of old trains in a Wisconsin museum, I saw a small platform on the front of the engine to which the cow-catcher was attached, and said to myself, "so that's how he did it."

In 1956, Ed Witte was elected president of the American Economics Association. The following year, at the age of 70, University rules required that he retire. I believe my doctoral dissertation, accepted in 1957, was the last one he sponsored.

After he retired, he took a teaching job in Michigan. I saw him one last time at a conference in Chicago. We sat in a restaurant and talked. He wanted to know if the job I had taken with the Federal Reserve in Philadelphia was OK, and whether I liked it. A short time later, I met a disaffected faculty colleague of Witte's in Philadelphia. He told me that the students at Michigan had complained about Witte–too many opinions, too many anecdotes, not enough rigor. Then, in 1960, he died.

The years after passed quickly for me, working in Washington, teaching in New York, marriage and family. On occasion I would look at the books I had salvaged from the stack he discarded when he retired. I reread his congressional testimony as Executive Director of the President's Council on Economic Security in 1935; and thought about how well he dealt with the questions of unfriendly congressmen who seemed to think the title "professor" was a pejorative term.

While my daughter was in college at Macalester, she spent one weekend in Madison. When she told me she had stayed at the Edwin Witte Residence Hall, memories came rushing back Well, I thought, isn't that something. They named a residence hall for Ed

Witte. A number of years later, when I returned to Madison after an absence of 48 years, I found a plaque on Bascomb Hill by the entrance to the Law School that commemorated Edwin Witte as the author of the Social Security Act, the most significant legislation produced by Franklin Roosevelt's New Deal — legislation that had contributed more to improving the lives of Americans than any other 'New Deal' measure.

I was elated by the recognition he had received for his contribution to a beleaguered generation, and to its progeny, of which I am one. He had ridden his cow-catcher beyond Milwaukee with fortitude and wisdom to a higher ground of national accomplishment. I took some pride in that he was a man with whom, in my mind, I had been working with only the day-before-yesterday.

In Chicago, You Can Freeze to Death in the Winter

An arctic wind blew across Lake Michigan, filled the air with white flakes and whipped around buildings and through crosswalks. Pedestrians moved carefully along the streets, clutching their hats and bracing themselves, grabbing the occasional railing or tree along their way. They sheltered from time-to-time in the entrances to buildings.

I was a graduate student at the University of Wisconsin. Chicago felt even colder than Madison, about 90 miles northwest. Madison didn't have wind whipping off Lake Michigan; its lakes were frozen, and somehow the days seemed brighter, even at 10 below zero.

I had been employed by Corwin Edwards, then a Professor at the University of Chicago. He had been chief economist at the Federal Trade Commission. He was writing a book on the effects of recent Supreme Court decisions that struck down price-fixing among producers of corn syrup in selling to candy manufacturers and others. The book was to be published by the Brookings Institution. I had been hired to interview corporate officials whose firms had been involved. The pay was a welcome supplement to my fellowship stipend. Most importantly, it exposed me to the ideas of a notable economist in my field of interest, and helped me gain a better understanding of issues I was addressing in my doctoral dissertation.

On this cold, wintery day in Chicago, I was on my way to meet an official in the Williamson Company, maker of the O'Henry candy bar, known in the trade as a 'nut role.' Driving to the Williamson office in Chicago was not easy. The snow-covered streets were clogged with traffic. Cars moved erratically, sometimes sliding on unseen ice. I tried to slow, when necessary, with as much foresight as possible. Using the brake pedal was a last resort, likely as not to cause a skid as to bring the car to a stop. Even a minor accident would mean getting out in the frigid weather, exchanging information with a disturbed stranger, and maybe the police. An accident would also make me late for my appointment.

A stressful half-hour of driving brought me to the Williamson building. It was a a short distance from a large hotel with a gaudy canopy, and a doorman who was dressed like Russian royalty. The doorman seemed miserably cold as he ushered people clutching their coats through the revolving entrance door, calling bellboys to deal with luggage and whistling down cabs. Thankfully, the hotel parking lot was open to the public. I walked from the parking lot into the warmth of the Williamson office building.

The official I met was happy to talk about the changes brought about by the Court's decision. He told me how his company had been affected, and what he believed had been the impact on his suppliers, customers and competitors. He asserted that the O'Henry bar would thrive in the post-decision environment because it was better than the other nut roles. "Peanuts, fudge and caramel, covered in milk chocolate," he declared; "it isn't just a candy bar, it's a food." He was scathing in his remarks about O'Henry's principal rival, Baby Ruth. "It has no chocolate," he told me, "none at all. Look at the ingredients on the wrapper – only cocoa butter." When I asked him a question he didn't want to answer, he simply said he couldn't talk about it. But, at one point, he left the room, saying he'd be back in a minute, leaving in plain sight a paper with the information he couldn't talk about. "O'Henry," I thought, "speaks in many ways."

When the interview was over, he thanked me for coming, and said he would like to see the study when it was completed. I assured him he would. He handed me a large wrapped package,. "A gift," he said.

I left his office, took the elevator to the lobby, and out into windswept Chicago. "A good day's work," I told myself. "No car accidents, a useful interview, and a gift." When I got to my car, I opened the package. It was a box full of O'Henry candy bars. Candy bars, hell! It looked like food to me.

A Bad Day in November

We walked along Pennsylvania Avenue, past the White House and the Executive Office Building on a brisk Autumn day. Our own offices were in the Treasury, the granite structure with a statue of Alexander Hamilton in front. In our brief time in Washington, we had learned to avoid its cafeteria, a haven for rodents, beetles and other unwelcome guests. We turned left on 17th Street, heading for the newly-constructed offices of the FDIC and its spotless top-floor lunch room. There, we could look out through the large near ceiling-to-floor windows to Constitution Avenue, the Washington Monument surrounded by its grassy mall, and beyond to the Potomac River shimmering in the sun.

I was with a group that had come to work with a recently appointed Comptroller of the Currency, the Treasury official who supervised national banks. The new Comptroller was a charismatic man for whom the lights seemed brighter when he entered a room. He was also a maverick who aimed to shake things up in a banking industry that had been traumatized by the thousands of failures during the 1930s. Bankers had become comfortable with government restrictions that accepted monopolistic practices and suppressed competition. He introduced new measures designed to promote competitive behavior. Doing so earned him numerous enemies in the Washington bureaucracy and in congress.

Our lunchtime discussion centered on his most recent provocation. By statute, the Comptroller was a member of the three-person board that managed the FDIC. He had antagonized the other two members by refusing to attend meetings, arguing against the FDIC's protective approach to the banks whose deposits it insured. It was rumored the FDIC was going to ban the Comptroller's staff from their building. The potential loss of a good place to eat was tempered by our pleasure in our boss' irreverent behavior.

After lunch, we walked back for the Treasury, talking about a journal we were preparing to publish and the articles we needed. On entering the building, we had our first indication that something was wrong. I found a group huddled around a radio, talking about a motorcade in Dallas. A secretary told me that President Kennedy had been shot and that he had been rushed to the hospital. She didn't know what his condition was.

We waited, overcome by a multitude of concerns. Will he recover? Will he be incapacitated? When will we know? Who could have shot him? Why? Will Lyndon Johnson have to assume the Presidency? What effect will this have on Kennedy's policies and his legislative agenda? How will it affect the Comptroller? How will it affect our jobs? There had been an attempt on Harry Truman's life that failed. There had been an attempt to kill Franklin Roosevelt in Florida that resulted in the death of Anton Cermak, the Mayor of Chicago. McKinley, Garfield and Lincoln had been assassinated. We all hoped Kennedy would be alright.

I sat in my office, looking out the window at the White House. After some time, I saw a man emerge from a door on the roof. In my mind, he will always be a small man, but perhaps it was only the distance. He walked to the pole that held the American flag and lowered it to half-mast.

I left the office and walked to my bus stop. I went home to my apartment in Arlington and to my wife, eight months pregnant with our first born. The events that followed are blurred in my memory. Oswald was captured; I saw Jack Ruby shoot him on live television. My wife and I stood on the sidewalk by the Treasury Building watching soldiers march, the caissons roll, and a lone horse leading a wagon with the hearse, followed by the dead President's wife. We mourned for Kennedy, and for ourselves.

The world heaved and moved on. The Comptroller who had been a favorite of the President and greatly admired by his staff had antagonized too many people. He was forced to leave a year or so later. Most of us who had come in response to his initiatives found other jobs. In the years that followed, the Vietnam war escalated, others prominent leaders were assassinated, cities burned and Watergate collapsed a presidency.

What if Kennedy not gone to Dallas, or his motorcade taken a different route, or what if Oswald had missed. I know enough of chaos theory and Robert Frost's poetry "how way leads on to way" to understand that things would have been different. Would they have been better? Mathematics and poetry are silent on this question. All I can say for certain is that a bad day in November filled me with remorse.

Minsky, Mayer and Me

Martin Mayer, an accomplished financial journalist, and an author who had written best-selling books about banking and the Federal Reserve was in process of writing what would probably be his last book when he died, a biography of the influential, but idiosyncratic economist, Hyman Minsky. Mayer, himself, was a unique personality. Testifying alongside him before a congressional committee, I recall him presenting himself by saying:

"My name is Martin Mayer. I live by my wits."

Of Minsky, he wrote: *Natura il fece, e poi ruppe la stampa*, quoting an early 16th Century Italian poet, and roughly translated as "nature made him and then broke the mold." Before Martin died, he left me a surprise.

~ ~ ~ ~

At a conference in the late1950s, someone, I'm not sure who, pointed to a large man sitting in the bar of the conference hotel and whispered in my ear, "that's Hy Minsky;" a rugged face set off by an abundance of hair in a rumpled suit. "He writes interesting articles about the financial system." I had no idea who Minsky was. However, I had an article of my own to write on the financial outlook for the monthly *Business Review* of the Federal Reserve Bank of Philadelphia. I thought I might take a look at some of Minsky's work.

His analysis of how money markets had developed since the war, and the role of central banks in the new environment, was provocative. He described a developing threat to the financial system. His paper was written for academic economists; mine had to be accessible to a non-professional audience. Ignoring technical details, I adopted some of his ideas, added thoughts of my own, and simplified for a wider audience. The article was well received.

A few years later, I met Minsky in Washington, at the Office of the Comptroller of the Currency where one of his papers was to be included in a book the Office was publishing. His paper was titled

"Can It Happen Again?" Everyone understood what he meant by 'It.' He was asking whether another 'Great Depression,' like the one that had devastated the nation in the 1930s, could occur. Minsky believed it could. The economists in the office who were editing the book, along with most economists at that time, thought the likelihood bordered on zero. We had corrected the mistakes of the past, installed automatic stabilizers, like unemployment insurance; and we knew how to shape government policies to prevent disasters. They laughed at Minsky, but published his article anyway.

After that, I moved to the Federal Reserve in Washington and had occasion to spend time with Minsky. I was working on a study the Board had undertaken of its lending policies at the discount window, both in normal times and when banks got into serious trouble. I suggested that Minsky, who was teaching at Washington University in St. Louis, was someone who could help as an academic consultant. I and the head of the study ran the suggestion by the Director of the Research Division, who asked, "Why do you want 'Chicken Little?' We laughed. We hired him anyway.

I got to talk with Minsky while he was at the Board. He had grown up in New York during the depression, somehow found his way to the University of Chicago and Harvard. He was engaging, had uncommon ideas, was fearless in propounding them, and had a droll sense of humor. He suggested, tongue-in-cheek, that a bank charter was a license to steal; and that many young people joined protest movements (it was the sixties) because the sex was better.

He was, however, dead serious about the fragility of the economy, swinging precariously between prosperity and collapse. It was during his time at the Federal Reserve Board in Washington that he developed his 'financial instability hypothesis.' Some of what he wrote was incomprehensible to the people who had to pass on it. To the relief of those who had approved his hiring, I provided an intelligible summary.

As the economy became more volatile toward the end of the 1970s, Minsky became better known outside the economics profession. The *New Yorker* labeled the financial upheaval that occurred in the early 1980s "a Minsky Moment." Newspapers picked up on the term and kept repeating it every time a serious downturn or financial crisis developed. No one was laughing anymore.

We remained friends after I left the Board for a teaching position in New York and I would see him from time-to-time He invited me to meetings in St. Louis, I met his wife and young child. When he retired, he became a distinguished scholar at the Levy Economics Institute of Bard College. He spent part of his year in Italy, where his wife had a home in Bergamo. He graciously acknowledged my help in forwards to several of his books, parts of which I reviewed in draft, He asked me to speak at a conference in Sienna.

Minsky died in 1996 at the age of 77, leaving a small but enthusiastic following. As a prophet and explainer of the economy's fragility, a characteristic that has revealed itself over the last 50 years, some believe he should have received a Nobel prize.

~ ~ ~ ~

Martin Mayer, in the course of his research on Minsky, asked if I would meet with him. He wanted to know how Minsky had come to thank me in forwards to his books. I described how we had met, his work at the Board and our subsequent relationship. A year or so later, Martin delivered a report on his progress to a conference at the Levy Institute. To my complete and everlasting surprise, he told his audience that:

> "The most important person in Minsky's career was Bernard Shull...I talked to him the other day. . . . He was a young member of the research staff at the Philadelphia Fed when he read Hy's original article on central banks and the money market...."

I never thought about my relationship with Hy Minsky that way. He was a well-known economist when I met him who had materially added to our understanding of how the economy worked. But I'll accept Martin's judgement, having, in my youthful exuberance, 'cast some bread upon the water' after meeting up with Minsky and his thought-provoking ideas a very long time ago.

IV

RELATIVES, FRIENDS AND OTHERS

I have met and worked with some well-known people including Nobel prize winning economists and others who were worthy of the honor, high level appointed government officials and congressmen before whose committees I've testified. But among the most memorable have been relatives, friends and, sometimes, casual acquaintances.

Joe

Joe was born in Richmond in 1903, the oldest boy in an immigrant family with five children and little money. His mother died when he was 10. After his father remarried, Joe felt compelled to protect his younger sister from a stepmother who favored her own child. The rest of his life he felt a need to protect someone, usually female.

His father moved the family to Philadelphia to be closer to relatives and in search of a better life. Joe left school after the 6th grade. He found a job with Western Union, delivering telegraph messages on a bicycle. He learned to box, and fought some as an amateur. He ultimately found his way into the movie business—as a motion picture projectionist. He ran film and managed spots for the vaudeville acts that performed in the theaters where he worked. When he decided he was earning enough, he married and started a family.

Joe was employed most of his working life in a movie house in center city Philadelphia that ran one-hour shows. These included newsreels and short subjects: *Paramount News*, *The March of Time*, travelogues and cartoons. During World War II, the one-hour shows attracted people who had an hour or so to spend, waiting for a bus, waiting for a train, waiting for something.

Outside the confines of the projection booth, Joe's passion was walking. He would frequently walk the 6 or 7 miles from his home to work, through Fairmount Park, by the Zoo, over the Schuylkill River, past the Art Museum, and down the Benjamin Franklin Parkway. In winter, he walked briskly, clapping his hands together when they got cold, like the long-coated traffic cops on street corners. Reaching center city, he would turn into a small alley. Half-way down a large metal door gave back entrance to his movie house. Opening the door, he'd walk up a flight of metal steps to the protective warmth of the projection booth where he put in 8-to-12 hour shifts.

Throughout his life, Joe was honest to-a-fault. He believed that behind every great fortune was a criminal act. His children assumed that was why they weren't rich. He paid their college tuition out-of-pocket rather than accept a political scholarship from a friendly ward leader; he thought the proffered gift was unethical.

Joe developed distinctive ideas about political affairs, learning some from the newsreels he was running. When it came to politics, he was prescient. He was certain in 1948 that Harry Truman would defeat Dewey, when everyone knew Truman didn't stand a chance. Truman's election convinced friends, neighbors and his children that he knew things others didn't know. His wife remained skeptical,

Somewhere, somehow Joe also developed an appreciation for literature. He liked the English romantic poets. He revered Lincoln's "Gettysburg Address." He purchased a set of the 100 Greatest Books, he said for his children. They came bound in fancy leather with a mahogany bookcase large enough to hold them all. There was Melville's *Moby Dick*, the works of Caesar and Cicero, Silas Marner, *She* by J. Haggard Rider and the poetry of Percy Bysshe Shelly. Joe was partial to "The Cloud," a poem he liked to recite.

I am the daughter of Earth and Water
And the nursling of the Sky
I pass through the pores of the ocean and shores
I change, but I cannot die

Later in his life, when his movie house began to show art films, Joe developed a liking for pictures like *The Red Shoes* and *Detective Story* with Kirk Douglas. Much later, when it switched to X-rated movies, like "Flesh Gordon," he retired.

I have a picture of Joe when he was about 13 or 14, posing by a brick wall with two other boys about the same age, in a fighting pose in front of an American flag flanked by college pennants, Harvard and Cornell. The picture was taken about the time America entered 'The Great War,' so the flag is understandable. Harvard and Cornell, beyond the boys' ken, are a mystery. But they all look fit and ready to take on the world. Joe also looks thoughtful; even then he appears to know things that others didn't know.

Joe came to age at a time when earning a decent living, owning your own home, providing for your family and advancing your children's lot were, for most men of his background, the focal points of ambition. Reflection, self-knowledge and 'following your bliss' were luxuries outside their understanding. Joe died when he was 93, long after his younger sister, and after his only daughter and then his wife. Like his treasured 'Cloud,' he might have lived forever, but there was no one left to protect.

Bill

Bill had a lot going for him. He was good looking, energetic, charming, self-confident and very smart. My mother's younger brother, he grew up poor in Philadelphia but was determined to rectify that. He was the first in the family to go to college. He got a Masters degree in Economics. However, he graduated in the middle of the Great Depression; and the only job he could get was as a stock boy in a liquor store. He joined the communist party, bent on the redistribution of wealth. But his enthusiasm for radical change faded after a few years when the leaders of his group threw him out of the party because he asked too many questions.

My first memories of Bill were when he came to see me on a cold, rainy day. I was about 6 years old and sick with some childhood disease. He was in his mid-20s. I liked him. Over the next few years, he took me to movies, had a picture of us taken by a sidewalk photographer and talked about political issues that he insisted were neglected in my school books. Later, when I was about 12 or 13, he began giving me books to read: college texts on the history of the United States, Lincoln's Steffan's *Autobiography* that told about how he uncovered political corruption in the early 20th Century, and Sidney and Beatrice Webb's *History of Trade Unionism*.

Bill's career breakthrough came when war broke out in 1941. He was employed by the War Labor Board in Washington. I visited Bill and his wife, traveling on a train, for the first time, by myself.

I have never forgotten war-time Washington, with its temporary wooden buildings off the mall, its swarming crowds on every street, uniformed soldiers and sailors everywhere. I saw the Capitol and the White House. Bill took me to the top of the Washington Monument. I was disappointed on Sunday when I found that the paper he got, the *New York Times*, had no comics.

Bill came back to Philadelphia after the war to a new, prestigious position in labor relations with a large, drug store chain. After a few years, he left the company to start his own 'investigations' business. It involved placing agents in stores and warehouses to check for theft that the firms that hired him saw as rampant.

Bill did not do well as a 'private eye.' Apparently crime paid, but not crime detection. He did better as an arbitrator in labor disputes. His intelligence, street-wise insights, and toughness made him a natural. I remember riding with him as he drove to various locations with a car-load of Christmas gifts for clients. One, a well-known Mafia figure with whom he had some rapport, was a power in the Teamsters. He told Bill that until the age of 10, he thought his name was "Shut Up."

It was real estate, however, that provided Bill with what he was after. He took me to meetings where he persuaded doctors, lawyers, and others to invest with him. They wanted higher returns than they could earn on government securities, but with comparably low risk. Bill persuaded them that real estate syndication met their expectations. Years later, I inferred that similar 'wants' motivated many of those who lost money with Bernie Madoff.

Bill changed gradually, but noticeably. As he became successful and grew wealthy, he seemed to become angrier and more vindictive. He erupted when he thought people were taking advantage of him, which was often. Along with a large house in an exclusive main-line area of Philadelphia, he acquired Brutus, the most ferocious dog I had ever seen–a giant Schnauzer who had a particular dislike for mailmen. Brutus was impervious to mace; Bill was indifferent to lawsuits. After he lost a child to suicide, he left his wife of many years to live with a woman who didn't seem very much different.

I was sorry when Bill died. I understood the arc of his life, and still marvel at it: from wanting a job, to wanting to change the world, to wanting to be rich; and from poverty to wealth; from socialist to capitalist; from 'good guy' to gargoyle. He was a tsunami of 'creative destruction.'

Bill came to me in the rain when I was 6 and, as the saying goes, went with the wind. Friends still ask me about him. I tell them that Bill passed this way, and I miss him.

Jack

His parents anointed him J. C. and told him to choose his own first name. He chose "Jack." I first met Jack when he came from Texas with his wife, JoAnn, and a 2-year-old daughter to work as an economist at the Federal Reserve Bank in Philadelphia. Jack was tall and thin with an abundance of energy. He was bursting with unusual ideas that sometimes sounded dopey, but often weren't. At first, I wasn't sure whether Jack and I would be colleagues or competitors. But any tension evaporated when, not long after he arrived, we attended a conference and he asked to borrow a shirt. I decided that if he could bum a shirt, we would be friends. Don't ask about the logic.

Jack was a natural-born gambler. His father had been an itinerant newspaper man in Texas who wildcatted for oil on the side. He never found any but saw others get rich overnight." That's what Jack had in mind, to get rich overnight. He would periodically buy two-dollar stocks through an 'undocumented' broker, watch it skyrocket, and hold on until it fell below the price he paid. He never got upset; he always believed he would make it back.

Jack once responded to an ad in the Wall Street Journal placed by someone who wanted to sell a gold mine. He called the number listed and told me he talked to a man who sounded as if he was in a telephone booth at a railroad station. The mine, it turned out, hadn't been worked since the end of World War II and was filled with water. I passed. So did he. But Jack's instincts were dead-on. The price of gold had been fixed at $35 an ounce at the time. Since then it has skyrocketed.

During the Cuban missile crisis in 1962, Jack and I were designated by the Bank to go to a relocation center in the mountains when the threat level rose one more step. What we were to do when we got there was never made clear; I think it involved distributing money after the expected nuclear exchange destroyed the banking system. We were told not to bring our families.

While we waited, Jack loaded his Volkswagen Beetle with

canned food, toilet paper and a shotgun. He had JoAnn, with their baby in tow, drive to a motel near the relocation center and wait for him. He asked if Janice, my wife of all of about 6 months, wanted to go with JoAnn. In those days, however, Janice had no time for Armageddon. She couldn't go, she said, because she had a cold. The crisis ended and JoAnn returned after a few dismal days in the mountains.

Thereafter, fortune smiled on Jack, at least for a while. He moved to higher-paying jobs at commercial banks. A decade later, he had become the chief investment officer of a large bank in Cleveland, with prospects of becoming president. When Janice and I visited his home in Chagrin Falls, he put us up in a private wing of his massive estate.

But fate is fickle. In the early 1980s, interest rates reached double digits and the prime rate exceeded 20 percent. Jack devised a scheme that would earn his bank millions if rates fell quickly. They didn't; his bank lost millions and he lost his job. The next time we visited, food was in short supply. He told me he had mortgaged his property to invest in oil drilling rigs. Then, the market for oil collapsed, taking the rigs with it. JoAnn told us she didn't know what she would do if they lost their house. They did.

Later, Jack called me to say he was on his way to Costa Rica to meet an old friend from Texas who offered him a job. He told me his friend had been barred from returning to the United States, I think for fomenting a revolution in some central American country. I lost track of Jack after that. But I wouldn't have been surprised if he'd made and lost several fortunes since we last talked.

I heard from him for the first time in two decades a few years ago. He told me he had been in Costa Rica all this time and that he had done well. He sent a picture of the grand house in which he was living and invited me to visit? I asked if he ever got back to the United States? He told me he was living in the mountains where no one could find him. That was the last I heard from Jack. Janice doesn't want to go to Costa Rica, anymore than she wanted to go to the mountains during the Cuban missile crisis.

There's a Tom Russell song about a gambler who 'throws horseshoes at the moon.' "Sometimes ya hook the milky way or the outstretched hands of God. But mostly they just fall into a dark and dusty hole...." Jack has always thrown horseshoes at the moon.

We all throw horseshoes, but mostly at targets a lot closer. I hope this time J. C. has hooked the milky way, or better yet the outstretched hands of a generous God who, just in case, has a shirt or two to spare.

Jake, Lyla and a Martin Guitar

Wandering through libraries and bookstores has always been my delight. So it was not unusual, shortly after my retirement, to be browsing through the books on the remainder table of a now gone, and almost forgotten, Borders bookstore. My attention was drawn to a coffee-table book on the history of guitars and, in particular, to one page that pictured a trendsetting Martin guitar that President Herbert Hoover had given to a White House guest in 1932. I was stunned by its resemblance to my own guitar, an instrument I had purchased and played a half-century before while a graduate student at the University of Wisconsin. I had long ago banished it, wrapped in its torn, cloth gig bag, to a dark, unheated closet. The image in the book struck a chord that resonated, It carried me back to another time and place.

Meeting Jake

Jake joined us at a large, round wooden table in *Der Rathskeller* of the Memorial Union. It was the Fall of 1955. He was thin, pale with a receding hair-line, and older than the other grad students with whom I was sitting. He was, he told us, a biochemist or a biophysicist, I'm not sure which; but he had been working on photosynthesis, and was employed in one of the labs on campus. He told us he was interested in folk music, played a banjo and was looking for someone who played guitar. I had a $5 dollar guitar with f-slots. I could play a few chords and knew the words to "John Henry." We got together a few days later in his apartment. He introduced me to his wife Lyla, a slim, bright light of a woman with long black hair whose family had emigrated from India. She would sing with us.

Jake picked up a guitar, played a little, and then began to play the banjo. I had a lot to learn about the playing the guitar. We decided to meet once-a-week. He taught; I learned enough. Others gathered round. They came with guitars, harmonicas, mandolins, fiddles and flutes. One showed up with a musical saw that produced the most sorrowful sound I had ever heard. One of Lyla's friends played the sitar.

As my playing improved, I found that my $5 guitar simply wasn't good enough. Jake offered to help me find a better one. One Saturday morning we drove to Milwaukee in his car, an ancient black limousine that had once been a hearse. Walking through pawn shops, Jake singled out an old guitar with a marred finish and that was worn around the pick guard. The steel strings were too high, making it painful to hold them down. But it was a Martin with a deep bass, bright treble and a great sound. The price was $30. Living at the time on the modest generosity of the University, I borrowed most of the money from Jake.

Martin in hand, reinforced by Jake and Lyla, I volunteered to provide entertainment for the Economics Department's Christmas party. Jake, Lyla and I played and sang, Civil War and Great Depression songs, and Woody Guthrie on building the Grand Coulee Dam. We received a wild ovation. My economic theory professor, naturally dour and always contentious, accused me of bringing in ringers from the Music Department. I told him it was the Physics Department.

Jake was plugged into the folk music scene, such as it was before Bob Dylan, Peter, Paul and Mary, Joan Baez and the revival of the 1960s. But there were signs. We drove to Chicago one night to hear Odetta sing to a sold-out audience at the Gate of Horn. Jake knew Pete Seeger who, during his blacklisted years, played the college circuit. He threw a party for Pete the night before he performed in Madison. Regretfully, I couldn't make it. 'Preliminary exams' began the next morning, a grueling five days of writing answers to questions five hours a day. The next year Jake and Lyla moved to California. I left Wisconsin for Philadelphia.

~ ~ ~ ~

In the years that followed, I lost touch with Jake and Lyla; graduate school faded in the wake of career and family life. But it all came back when I saw the picture of the old Martin at Borders. I didn't know it at the time, but my plunge into reminiscence would set me off on a journey of discovery, finding out about the old guitar, and looking for Jake. When it was done, I was astonished and more than a little shaken.

The Guitar

Was the guitar I kept in a closet for 50 years valuable? The picture I found in the book in Borders seemed to suggest it might be. I began my efforts to find out by determining when the guitar was made. The Martin Company's website provides a table of serial numbers for all the guitars it has produced since 1898. With flashlight in hand, I inspected the braces inside the body of my guitar and found an inscribed number. Taking the number to the Martin website, I found it had been made in1931.

My next step, in trying to find what it was worth, was to take the guitar to Jeff Kline's music store in Lambertville, not far from my home. Lamberville is a river-front town across the Delaware from the better-known New Hope, just a few miles north of where Washington crossed the Delaware on Christmas night in 1776 to surprise the British and the Hessians in Trenton. It is now a Mecca for tourists and overrun by antique stores.

Jeff's store is reached by walking though an ice cream parlor, and then climbing a steep flight of stairs. I found him with an entourage of familiars amid a clutter of string instruments of varying ages and quality and condition.

Jeff examined my guitar and told me it was an OM 28, the 'OM' standing for Orchestra Model. It was a type Martin had stopped producing a long time ago. One of the bystanders asked if she could play the guitar. Left-handed, she turned it upside down and began filling the room with driving melodies. "There's still a lot of life in that guitar," another onlooker declared. He told me he was a collector and offered to buy the guitar at what seemed an outrageous price. Jeff said he would make an offer if I was prepared to sell. I told them both I wanted to hold on to it.

Jeff suggested I could get a decent idea of its value by contacting a music store in Philadelphia that had advertised a similar guitar. When I inquired, I found the store was asking double the amount offered by the collector.

Knowing what the Philadelphia music store was asking for its guitar, convinced me that the Martin I owned should be insured. But, for insurance, I would first need an appraisal. Searching for someone to appraise it, a music store in Princeton recommended the Mandolin Brothers on Staten Island, an establishment with a national reputation for providing musical instruments to well-known performers. I phoned and, to my surprise, my call was answered by Stanley Jay, the owner of the store. I told him about my guitar, what I had found out and my interest in getting an appraisal. His response was: "Am I going to have the opportunity to visit with this instrument?" I assured him he was.

The Mandolin Brothers was housed in an undistinguished stone building with barred windows in a commercial section of Staten Island. Inside, the walls were adorned with guitars, banjos and mandolins. Instruments were standing upright on the floor and laid out on tables. I later learned that the shop's famous clientele included Bob Dylan, Paul McCartney, and Paul Simon. Joni Mitchell referred to it in one of her songs. Chris Thiele purchased a 1924 mandolin there, spending a substantial portion of his McArthur genius grant.

When I walked in, Stanley Jay looked at the guitar and called his 'luthier.' "Leroy, come on up. I want you to see a very important instrument." Leroy came up from what I imagined was his basement workshop, examined the guitar, but said nothing. Stanley told me the guitar I had was an innovation in 1931, with 14 instead of 12 frets on the neck. It was made of Brazilian cherry and Adirondack spruce, with a mahogany neck and an ebony fingerboard. Only a small number had been made.

He also told me the neck had sprung and that was why the strings were high. He was reluctant to undertake the repair unless I permitted him to sell the guitar on consignment. I told him I wanted to keep it for a while. He said, "I'll leave it up to Leroy." Leroy finally spoke. He said he would like to work on the guitar.

The work took time, requiring the neck to be separated from the body. When I called after 5 months to see how it was going, Leroy, still a man of few words, said "nearly done."

I asked: "Have you played it?"

He had.

"How did it sound?"

"Monstrous."

The repaired guitar, light as a feather, had become easy on the fingers and a joy to play. It had a resonance I had never before appreciated.

A few years later, I brought the guitar to the Martin factory in Nazareth, Pennsylvania for a minor repair. A Martin official expressed delight in my aged example of his company's excellence; I took the opportunity to ask about the thinning wood below the pick guard.

"Is there anything I can do about it?"

"Not unless you want to reduce the guitar's value," he responded, "and possibly the quality of its sound."

"What if the wood wore away completely?

"Then," he cheerfully told me, "you would have a guitar with a hole in it, like Willie Nelson's. We've been trying to get him to bring his in for years, but he refuses."

~ ~ ~ ~

I had, with considerable satisfaction, uncovered the provenance of my guitar and improved its condition. But I also wanted to find Jake, to let him know about the instrument he had helped me purchase a half-a-century before. Tracking down the guitar had a happy ending. Tracking down Jake, did not.

Looking for Jake

Where was Jake? My daughter, Abby, took up the search using the most fiendish device for invading privacy ever invented–the internet. Early on she located a record of Jake's marriage to Lyla Ghose in Urbana, Illinois in 1951. She also found mention of Jake's activities as a respected member of a scientific research group, looking for a way to harness photosynthesis, the process by which plants make use of the energy from sunlight. The group was led by Eugene Rabinowitch, a biophysicist who had worked on the atomic bomb, and was the first editor of the *Bulletin of Atomic Scientists*. An admiring memoir written about Rabinowitch and his group noted Jake's contribution in 'crystallizing chlorophyll, and discovering the red shift of the absorption band.' It also remarked on the 'fun he brought to the intellectual life of the lab with his banjo playing.' Jake had published articles in prestigious journals, and presented papers at international conferences.

His current whereabouts, however, were a mystery. A former colleague confirmed that Jake had taken a position at Stanford, but wrote that "...we don't know where he is now." Another said that Jake had "...suddenly disappeared from Stanford without leaving any word with anyone...."

Finding Lyla proved easier. She had worked in California for Linus Pauling and his wife Ava Helen, probably as a transcriber. But she had divorced Jake in 1970, and died in 1972 at the age of 43, the cause reported as 'barbiturate poisoning.' The picture that accompanied her death-notice was of the '30 something' Lyla I remembered, pretty, smart and completely self-assured. I found her death difficult to understand.

With Lyla gone and Jake in the wind, we pretty much gave up the search. Then, several years later, Abby discovered in April, 1974 newspaper articles the circumstances surrounding Jake's departure from Stanford. The articles were principally about the death of Barbara Ann (Nan) Goldie, a former debutante who had become a student radical at Stanford, and who had been missing for three years. Headlines in the Tri-City Herald of Pasco Washington reported "Three Sought in Probe of Woman's Death" and "Link Bones to Former Bay Radical." The police were probing "the grisly death" of Nan Goldie whose bones had been found scattered through debris in the Little Twin Lakes area of Washington, not far from the Canadian border. Nan Goldie had been identified through dental records

In April 1971, the 22-year-old Goldie checked into a motel near Spokane with her friend, Kristi Hinds, the daughter of the Dean of Students at Stanford; and with Hinds' husband, Earl Jacobs, a Stanford biophysicist. They stayed the night. The next morning, Jacobs was found dead from an overdose of sleeping pills. The police questioned the two women and let them leave, presumably for home. But they never got there, and there had been no sign of them since; that is, until Nan Goldie's bones were discovered three years later.

A reasonably coherent picture of Jake's tragic journey emerged from related articles. In the storm of student protests, campus violence and counterculture revolution that overtook the Stanford campus in the 1960's and early 1970s, Jake had divorced Lyla and married Kristi Hinds. He then left his faculty position without notice, effectively resigning from his career, and traveled with the two young women to a commune in British Columbia. Thereafter, for unknown reasons, they left the commune, traveled back across the border and fatefully checked into the Spokane area motel where Jake died. The two women departed the next morning and fell off the face of the earth.

~ ~ ~ ~

This story began with the picture of a guitar in a coffee-table book that brought back memories of meeting Jake in the student union of the University of Wisconsin. It ended with drug overdoses, an abrupt death in a motel room, missing women and bones strewn among the debris near Twin Lakes, Washington. It was hard for me to believe that what happened could have happened, to Jake and Lyla. Fifteen years earlier, they had been energetic, productive, full of good will and joy, warming the cold winter nights of Madison, Wisconsin with song and story. Through the years of lost contact, I had assumed that they were still around, somewhere, doing what they had always done. They weren't. Of the attachment I forged with them more than half-a-century ago, all that's left is the old Martin guitar that I bought with money borrowed from Jake. It still rings like a bell and mesmerizes. It brings Jake and Lyla to mind every time I pick it up. I should have sold it years ago. but I've found it hard to do.

Janice

I'll close this section with some things I've written for my wife, Janice. My underlying sentiments about her are captured in the few lines of an old Carter Family song.

"I'll ne'er forget where e're I roam,
wherever I may be
If ever I had a friend in this world,
you've been that friend to me"

A Sign along the Road

(For Janice on Her 75th Birthday)

In the distance beyond were
lakes and mountains, winding
roads, flowing rivers, fertile valleys
A sign by the road said "Scenic Drive,
this way." You said, let's see what's there.
We climbed a hill
A narrow path turned,
twisting through fields and trees
that blocked the sun along a sandy beach
birds of all design, swoop with song, turtle grass,
flowers bloom, deer lie still, creatures standing, sitting
marveling at the sights

Amazed and mystified
frightening and joyous things
you cry, I sing, here and there capturing
a world of magic, unexplained, winding on
through dark canyons, airy peaks, under points of light
passing by, passing through

Doesn't seem so long ago
we started down this unknown road
you reached out your hand, joined with me,
smiled in state of grace to see and feel what lay
ahead throughout an unknowable terrain, in lands beyond
we climbed a hill

Valentine Day Poems

Time Passes

You've grown old
(I haven't changed)
the wrinkles and the pains
tells me time has passed
but in your face, I still see
the same bright smile that captured me
and shined through all the tears
ballast in a roaring sea
of gain and loss and amity
together in the passing years

It's Valentine's Day Again

Another Valentine's Day and
and you were expecting a card, but there
were none that merited the $5.00 that is
now being charged for the demented sentiments
that are still being passed off as signs of affection
So here's my substitute. A thought
for you who are the last one I see
when I go to sleep at night and the first
when I wake in the morning

You are my Valentine, for now and forever
and that about covers it.

V

ABOUT NOW

The past lives like an electrical wire in some special memory compartment of the mind, sometime switching on and off. That compartment is the imminent destination of what follows in "About Now."

Walking in Barcelona

Barcelona is a beguiling city with a checkered past. Janice and I arrived on a cool, sunny day in June. I'd been interested in visiting Barcelona since I read George Orwell's *Homage to Catalonia* describing his experiences during the Spanish civil war that pretty much began and ended in Barcelona. I had also been working on a book that dealt with the development of modern banking. In the 14th Century, Barcelona was a financial center. Banks spurred trade and promoted growth. But they had problems not all that different from the kind of problems banks have today–they periodically failed. In 14th Century Barcelona, the authorities didn't bail them out. When a bank failed, the law decreed that the failed banker be disgraced by public crier, and detained on a diet of bread and water until all debts were satisfied. If they were not satisfied, the banker would be beheaded. In 1360, Francesh Castello was beheaded in front of his bank.

After we settled into our hotel, we began to walk the city streets and parks. We found the old section with its ancient cathedrals, the Roman ruins underneath, and the Picasso and Miró art museums. We walked La Rambla, saw the statue of Columbus on the

Mediterranean, for some reason looking East toward Italy. We walked the streets around Park Güell, so steep that the city had installed escalators next to the sidewalks; and we wandered through and wondered at breadth-taking Gaudi architecture.

One evening, as we walked along a pleasant street not far from the hotel, a young man approached. He asked, in heavily accented English, if we could tell him how to get to La Sagrada Família, Gaudi's unfinished church on which construction had begun in 1882, with completion now estimated for 2026. I stumbled through some directions. He thanked me and walked away.

Suddenly we were confronted by two older men who stopped us flashing badges; they identified themselves as police officers. One asserted they had observed me consorting with a known drug dealer. He insisted that I provide identification. We had, with forethought, left our passports and other important documents in the hotel safe. Janice, who they ignored, carried the credit cards and money. My wallet, had very little in it. I took it out and showed them a library card. Janice, with more presence of mind than me, asked to see their identification again. They waved their badges once more, and this time we looked more carefully. Without speaking we reached the conclusion that they had been purchased in a novelty store. We looked at them, each other, and silently walked away. One called after us, "Don't let it happen again." We paid no attention.

Maybe they were after money, maybe passports. We weren't sure. When we got to our hotel we told the manager what had happened and asked him to notify the police. He shook his head. "No," he said, "this is Barcelona!" Still seductive and with something that remains of the rough old Mediterranean seaport. But romantic imagery aside, shouldn't something be done about fake cops whose disreputable behavior tears at the social fabric, as well as the tranquility of tourists. Those impersonating police are at least as bad as failed bankers. Maybe we can start with 'disgrace by public crier and a diet of bread and water,' and go from there.

Driving to Naples

We leave mid-morning on New Year's Day. Everyone should be sleeping after the late-night celebration; traffic will be light.

Maybe in an alternate universe. In this one, everyone is awake and on the road. A multi-colored tapestry of cars and trucks, rising and falling with the undulating interstate, traveling 75-85 miles an hour. Daredevils tail-gate and weave in and out of the moving fabric, cross-stitching at high speed between the on-going cars.

I reflect on Travis McGee, John MacDonald's fictional private detective who lived at a marina in Fort Lauderdale on a houseboat called the Busted Flush, and who had a friend with a dog named Milton Friedman. I remember he once found himself driving on a freeway in Los Angeles, surrounded by fast-moving cars. His *modus operandi* was to 'get into the middle lane and keep up with the traffic.' You can learn a lot from Travis McGee.

Finally, the Welcome Center on Rt. 95 in Maryland. Welcome Centers are the true crossroads of America, where all races, religions, nationalities and generations meet to break bread and relieve themselves. Now on to Washington, around its beltway to the congestion on the road to Richmond. Cars slow to a stop-and-go crawl. The interstate is a parking lot.

At last, traffic is flowing freely. First night in Emporia Virginia. Something is wrong with the heat in our motel room. Midnight. Valerie comes up to fix the problem. I ask: "Valerie, do you know anything about this heating system." "Not really," she replies. I could call a repair man." "How long before he gets here?" "About two hours." "We have to be up at 6:00 am." "I won't charge for the room." We are warmed by the prospect of a free night at the Hampton Inn.

Early morning, on the road again. Billboard messages: "Norton's Vegetables--Pees to all...Turnip to the table." They bring back memories of Burma Shave that used to shower its wisdom along the highways in a succession of signs:

"Candidate says...Campaign Confusing...Babies kiss me...Since I've been using...*Burma-Shave*"

And

"Drinking drivers...Enhance their Chance...To highball home...In an ambulance...*Burma Shave*"

On to Brunswick, Georgia, and another motel. The forecast is for a winter storm. We wake up to a cold, cheerless morning; dark, low hanging, ice-laden clouds. The car's windshield is layered in ice. A young woman rushes from her post at the front desk to scrape the ice off with a credit card. It works. I file the technique and her consideration for future reference.

The radio tells us that driving is precarious. But the ice is melting and early morning traffic is light. Halfway to the Florida line, we realize that we left the Kindle in the motel room. We call; they have it; back we go. Now there's more traffic, and we begin to see multiple accidents. We flee South. Its only rain in Florida, no ice and little traffic. Driving is easy. Then the sun comes out. And so do other drivers. We come up behind a massive truck in the center lane, painfully passing another massive truck in the right-hand lane. An affront to the rules of the road, and a blow to Western civilization.

When we finally reach Naples, it's bitterly cold, with an arctic blast that further north has exploded into a "bomb cyclone." But none of this matters, as I imagine none of the headaches of 'getting there' mattered to Ponce de León when, 500 years ago, reputedly searching for the fountain of youth, he also arrived on the west coast of Florida–only to be tormented by its hostile residents. 'Such,' as the old song goes, 'are only slight diversions, and take not from the joy.'

The Beast of Pelican Marsh

The large side-by-side refrigerator in our rented condo in Pelican Marsh, a peaceful retreat in Naples, Florida, began to die late in the afternoon. It didn't simply wheeze, cough and shudder to a stop. It entered its end days with a slow dripping from the ice-maker inside the freezer. I placed a bowl underneath to catch the drip, and planned to call Marlene, our rental agent, in the morning. Later that evening, we found that the ice cream in the freezer had turned to soup. We called Marlene immediately. She promised to resettle our frozen vegetables in her own freezer and call a repair man in the morning. Though the freezer side of the side-by-side was kaput, the refrigerator side still seemed OK, continuing to belch out cold air. Janice and I went to sleep confident that the freezer would soon be fixed.

I was awakened the next morning by a mournful cry from the kitchen. Jumping out of bed, I heard Janice call out "all the food is ruined." The bread was alright, but the milk and cheese had gone bad. The refrigerator had died in the middle of the night. It was now just a warm body.

A repair man arrived later in the day. He looked and mumbled: "what a dinosaur." His verdict, "beyond repair. It's lost all its Freon; I could fry an egg on the coil. But," he added, "it isn't all bad. We can put in a new, better one in tomorrow. I'll call the owner, let him know."

This hopeful vision was soon shattered, replaced by Gerhardt, the owner's local *consigliere*. He told us the owner wanted to know why he needed a new refrigerator? "Why can't the lost Freon be replaced?"

"I have no idea," I replied. "Freon's an element that escapes me. Talk to the repair man."

Once convinced that the lost Freon could not be reinserted, the owner decided he didn't like the refrigerator proposed by the repair man. He would get his own. We were told, it would be about four days before a new one could be delivered. At this point, our intrepid agent, Marlene, stepped in. She called the owner and told him that "four days is too long; I'll give you two." The owner surrendered to the forces of good.

Gerhardt purchased the refrigerator for the owner; he didn't tell us from whom. Scheduled to arrive about 10:00 in the morning, it finally got to our condo on a flat-bed truck about 3:00 in the afternoon. A stainless steel, French door, bottom freezer, with ice-maker, water dispenser, a speaker system and digitalized controls; 6 feet high, 3 feet deep and 3 feet wide, 30+ cubic feet of steel, copper and plastic tubing, electrical wiring, and semiconductors. It was accompanied by two men, a forklift and a dolly. "How," I asked myself, "are these guys going to get it up the stairs to our 2d floor kitchen?"

Taking the old refrigerator out was relatively easy, even with a dolly that had a broken strap that threatened to put the old box into free fall. Getting the new one in, that by this time I had labeled 'The Beast,' was another story. The men disassembled all the parts they could–doors, shelves and bins–to be hauled up separately. Then the body of the beast and the agonizing shuffle up the stairs– "forget about the rugs, we'll take care of those later." Up they went, step by gruesome step.

About halfway up, the men straining to keep the refrigerator upright, a woman appeared on the driveway, screaming: "this truck is blocking my car; whoever heard of delivering a refrigerator this way; I'm calling the property manager; they could have demolished my Mercedes."

Marlene shrugged, "how gauche."

Gerhardt murmured, "Pay her no attention, we know this woman."

Around the bend the refrigerator went, then more stairs. One of the men, struggling, "careful I can't hold it!" Gerhardt came fast from behind to keep 'the beast' upright. Finally, the flat surface of the dining room floor. There was blood on the rug; one of the movers was limping. But the beast had landed.

The delivery men connected the wiring and plumbing, leveled the refrigerator and made it ready for use. Our ice cream became hard as a brick at 8 below zero. The beast hummed softly.

That night, around 3:00 in the morning, I was jarred awake by an ear-splitting screech that came from the kitchen. I jumped out of bed and rushed to the refrigerator. By the time I got there, the screeching had stopped.

I knew what it was and maybe what had happened! It was 'the beast,' adjusting to a new environment, proclaiming a new domain. Janice slept through it all; didn't hear a thing. She said that I probably had heard a bird. But I know what I know, and you can take it as a warning. Be wary of kitchen appliances with silicon chips and 'positronic brains.' They may not have devious intentions, but how can you be sure?

A Lament on Leaving Naples

I planned to write a novel, bizarre, surprising twists, hero
villain, mortal fear, tarnished family history, dark
menacing mystery you would
cheer

~ ~ ~ ~

it disappeared

I planned to write a poem, flint striking stone, fire
lighting up the sky erasing darkness
crescendo of inspired lines
to prize

~ ~ ~ ~

it vaporized

I planed to write a play, joy, distress, pain, pleasure
life, death, driven dialogue soaring to an
epilogue, a testament you'd
say

~ ~ ~ ~

they'll be a brief delay

Words replete for stories tie my mind in knots.
memories hold tight to that trouble-making lot.
Gone to hidden places, they promise to return
but who knows why and who knows when
the ever-loving cold wind
blows me back again

VI

SURVIVING THE FINANCIAL CRISIS

I spent the early years of my professional career with the Federal Reserve, first in Philadelphia and then in Washington. After leaving Washington for a teaching position in New York, I spent a good deal of my time talking and writing about the Federal Reserve. A remarkable federal agency, run by a relatively few appointed officials, names largely unknown, that 'creates money out of thin air' and can make the nation poor or prosperous. What lies below are pieces written in the wake of the financial crisis of 2008 and the economic decline that accompanied it. There are no footnotes.

Memories of Disaster

By the late 1950s, the ghosts of 'the Great Depression' had been all but banished; and so had the "D" word for economic declines. Believing we had found ways to moderate cyclical economic contraction, we substituted the word "recession" for when they occurred. An article written by Hy Minksy in the 1960s was titled "Can It Happen Again?" Everyone knew what 'It' was. In 2008, the sweeping economic disaster accompanying the financial crisis was called "the Great Recession" –the most serious economic collapse since 'It–' the 'D-word' was still not to be spoken.

A variety of ongoing economic problems and periodic disruptions, beginning in the 1970s, had given fair warning, that, despite the remedial measures that had been taken the economy was still vulnerable. Its vulnerability became a reality in 2008

For those who are very young, the financial crisis of 2008 may seem little more than a slasher film, with a pack of unknown villains, perhaps led by large banks, investment firms and insurance companies, topped off by Bernie Madoff cutting down wealthy investors. But those who remember the Great Depression of the 1930s, may well ask: "Isn't this where I came in?"

The 1930s was a decade of senseless loss that lingers just beneath conscious thought, waiting for a plausible reason to unroll its images, real or fanciful, of stock brokers jumping out of windows, depositors lining up in front of failing banks, haggard men and women in torn coats with drooping heads, in bread lines, living in shanty-towns, selling apples, hopping freight trains, going somewhere, getting away from wherever they were. Veterans marched on Washington, dispelled by tear gas, "Okies"left the dust bowl heading for the California fruit bowl, a panorama of desperation that filled those growing up with caution, and many who had grown up with remorse for not being cautious enough.

At least two developments have made the events of 2008 shockingly evocative. The first has been the destruction of the best and most respected names in business – a passage of blue chips to red ink. Who said, never bet against General Motors? Who could have imagined CitiGroup and Bank of America undone. Is it really true that Merrill Lynch, and Lehman Brothers no longer exist, the former as an independent entity, the latter, at all. And where have you gone, Wachovia, deliverer of dreams – to Wells Fargo, deliverer of mail.

The second invitation to memory has been the massive intervention by the Federal government. Hundreds of billions of federal dollars have been thrown into new programs and new "bail-outs" for old companies too important to fail. In the depression of the 1840s there had also been financial crisis. When business people and farmers couldn't pay their bills they bailed-out by default, went west placing signs on fence posts and doors of abandoned houses reading "Gone to Texas." Today, CEOs of major corporations could tack signs to their office doors reading "Gone to Washington."

We have not seen anything like the images of the Great Depression in 2008 or 2009, and it's unlikely that we will. Governments have a decent understanding of the mistakes they made in the 1930s, and are resolved not make them again. Treasury and Federal Reserve interventions saved us from 'It.' The problem, of course, is that in saving us from it, they create new problems. 'We never step into the same river twice,' and new economic disruptions, despite their appeal to memory, provide ample opportunity for new missteps.

Banking on Bail-Outs

Government bail-outs of banks "too-big-to-fail" are, as a general matter, reprehensible; but when catastrophe threatens, there seems little else to do. In 1796, the Bank of New York, one of a few banks that existed at the time, couldn't pay its debts and asked the Treasury for help. The Treasury Secretary, Oliver Wolcott, provided relief and the Bank survived. But even then, Wolcott knew there was a problem. In private he wrote "these institutions have all been mismanaged; I look upon them with terror. They are at present the curse, and I fear they will prove the ruin of the Government."

In May of 1984, Continental Illinois Bank of Chicago, one of the largest banks in the country at the time, was near collapse. The Federal Reserve supplied billions to replace the billions nervous depositors were withdrawing. It was just the beginning of what was to come.

The rationale for government 'bail-outs' has always been the belief that without aid the financial system might collapse. But it has never been clear that the damage bail-outs prevent is less than the damage they inflict.

Bailing-out a large and important bank means protecting it from failure. Its customers appreciate the fact that, in distress, the government is likely to step in. As a result, during prosperous periods, the likely-protected banks are able to attract funds more cheaply than those unlikely to be protected. This gives them a competitive edge over their smaller and less important rivals. The lower cost of funds encourages favored banks to reach out for riskier investments; and provides an incentive for other banks to grow by merger into favored status. Protection today encourages greater risk-taking that will require 'bail-outs' tomorrow.

Government officials, elected and appointed, have understood this for a very long time. In the wake of a crisis, they will invariably opt to prevent what they see as a possible collapse of the financial system, and look for other ways to meet the longer-term ramifications. Stung by a multitude of commercial and savings bank failures in the 1980s, Congress prohibited bail-outs in all but the most dire of circumstances–to the extent of requiring the President to certify the need. The Federal Reserve and other agencies have dodged the restraints, rationalizing "we had to do it." When it comes to possible system collapse "resistance is futile."

This doesn't mean that something can't be done before we reach the precipice. Some have suggested adjustments to bank capital to discourage risky behavior, and many have opted for better oversight by bank supervisors. Since the Continental Bank was bailed out, Congress has passed a number of comprehensive reform bills that have supposedly "modernized" bank regulation. It remains to be seen just how effective they will be. Historical perspective suggests that you not bet your house on it.

There is another answer that is likely too simple. Just don't let financial institutions reach a size that makes them 'too-big or too-important to fail.' Then we can let them fail, if they must, without catastrophe. Not that long ago, there was a political consensus in the United States that bigness in banking was dangerous. Laws passed in the 1950s blocked the new ways banks had found to circumvent old laws. But we've abandoned concerns about bigness on the dubious belief that growth, even to colossal size, is needed for banks to be efficient. Between the early 1980s and the financial crisis of 2008, over a quarter-of-a-century, the Federal Reserve approved every large bank merger that came before it.. Never once did it or any other Federal agency that reviewed bank merger cases, including the Justice Department, ever consider, even once, whether the merged banks would be "too-big-to-fail." In its recent bail-outs, moreover, the Treasury and the Federal Reserve facilitated large bailed-out banks to acquire other floundering financial institutions, making the survivors still larger.

It has now been over 200 years since Oliver Wolcott, felt it necessary to support the Bank of New York, and looked on it and other banks with terror. He believed they would be the ruin of the government. We've learned since then that it is not just the government that's at risk of ruin.

Paul Volcker and His 'Rule'

(With a nod to Peter Finley Dunne)

The Dodd-Frank Act that was a response to the financial crisis of 2008 contained provisions termed 'the Volcker Rule' that restricted banking organizations from engaging in the kind of speculative investments and relationships that it was believed contributed to the financial crisis of 2008.

"I see by the papers that Paul Volcker is in the news again," said McFadden as he stood behind the bar of Glass and Steagall's Silver Dollar Saloon.

"I thought he was dead," said Eccles, his long-time friend and customer.

"Not hardly," said McFadden. "He's lived through more financial nightmares than you and I can remember, enough for three lifetimes; but Paul is still with us."

"Is he, really?" said Eccles. "Well what's he up to now?"

"He's angry at the banks," said McFadden, "really angry. "They collapsed last year, and left the government holding the bag. Their top officers were so successful getting bail-out money that they're being rewarded with big bonuses. Paul says that isn't right. If they hadn't caused the collapse in the first place, the government wouldn't have needed to help them out."

"I thought," said Eccles, "the top bank officials explained that they were just serving the public."

"That's what they say, said McFadden, that their purpose is entirely *pro bono*. They want to take charge of as much money as they can get to keep it safe, where it won't suffer the indignities it would suffer if you and I were to hold on to some of it. But Paul isn't buying it."

"Well, I can see why he wouldn't, but what does he intend to do?"

"He intends to clamp down on the banks. He has a plan that the President calls 'the Volker Rule.' He knows we can't let them fly around on their financial trapeze without a safety net. The economy needs deposit insurance and the Federal Reserve to support financial institutions that gather deposits and lend to businesses and consumers, and cannot avoid, on occasion, running into trouble. But it doesn't need 'bail-outs.' The deposit insurance-Federal Reserve safety net creates what insurance people call a 'moral hazzard.' When banks are shielded against risk, they are likely to take on too much of it. That's why we need restrictions on what they can do, and supervisors to make sure they don't go too far.

The job is tough enough when banking is simple. When banks are allowed to buy and sell securities, create new ones, and trade for their own profit, things get pretty dicey. Paul says we can't let banks do that sort of thing. Others, like investment companies and hedge funds can take those kinds of risk, *but* without deposit insurance and Federal Reserve protection.

"I get it," said Eccles. "He wants banks who are protected to do less."

"Right," said McFadden. "And he doesn't want them to get bigger. He wants to stop the mergers before we end up with only two big banks that decide to join forces, they'll say, 'to reduce costs and increase competition.'

"Well, what do you think?" asked Eccles. "Is the Volcker rule going to work?"

"I don't know," said McFadden, "I have a lot of confidence in Paul. He killed inflation in the 1980s by raising interest rates to ungodly levels. He almost killed the rest of us doing it. As for his 'rule,' I think the devil will be in the details; so we'll see. But there's one thing I know for sure. If Paul has a rule, the bankers will find an exception."

Surviving the Financial Crisis at Books-a-Million

Have you been to one of the large bookstores recently, Barnes & Noble, Books-a-Million? The displays in these literary supermarkets suggest what the stores and publishers expect will sell: romance and detective novels, travel, home repair and self-improvement books, celebrity biographies, the classics (always on sale) and, of course, the remainder table, on the bargain aisle of broken dreams.

On a recent visit to one of these stores, the books that caught my eye were on a table in the business section – filled with "new arrivals" on the why's and wherefores of our economic woes, self-help nostrums for financial distress. How, I asked myself, did these guys get their books out so quickly? Do these books really have something to offer?

They claim they do. One batch promised to tell how bad the economy is: There was *IOUSA: One Nation under Stress, in Debt*, another was titled *The Foreclosure of America*, and then there were *The Two Trillion Dollar Meltdown* and *The End of Wall Street: As We Know It*. I got the message. Deep in debt, few could meet their payments, most faced foreclosure, perhaps whether or not they owned a house. As a result, financial markets had melted and Wall Street was terminal.

Other books identified the culprits, promised to name names, and to sort out the future. It was globalization according to *When Markets Collide*. It was perverse human behavior according to *Meltdown: How Greed and Corruption Shattered Our Financial System*. But maybe only on Wall Street according to *How Wall Street Caused the Mortgage and Credit Crisis*. Another meltdown book promised to tell the deregulation view of the Wall Street story: *Meltdown: A Free Market Look at Why the Stock Market Collapsed*. Then there was a book that foretold the bleak future and who was at fault: *The Great Depression Ahead and Chain of Blame*.

Just reading the titles and blurbs my understanding of the problem took a great leap forward. It was the greed and corruption of Wall Street, and maybe government regulation, that caused markets to collide, shattered our economy and brought on the melt down.

It was not, nevertheless, all hand wringing on the 'world-is-going-to-hell-in-a-hand-basket' table. There were titles that proclaimed salvation was only a purchase away. One promised to show *How to Prosper in Hard Times*; and another proclaimed *Game Over: How You Can Prosper in a Shattered Economy*. I particularly liked these titles: *The Little Book that Saves Your Assets; Smart Couples Finish Rich* and *The Finish Rich Dictionary*. I could take *The Ten Roads to Riches*; another suggested I might only need *9 Steps to Transforming My Relationship with Money*. But overall, I found my favorite in the admonition that *The First Billion is the Hardest*.

I doubt these books provide useful information; I find them as appealing as three card Monte. I suspect most of them will soon find the remainder table.

Strangely, the titles put me in mind of the Groucho Marx song "Lydia, the Tattooed Lady." Lydia's tattoos were like the cover of a book, or rather a whole library of books.

"On her back is the Battle of Waterloo,
Beside it the wreck of the Hesperus, too,
And proudly above waves the Red, White, and Blue,"
You can learn a lot from Lydia."

Despite the appeal of Groucho, I knew I wouldn't learn anything about the battles and wrecks advertised on Lydia's body, and I wouldn't learn anything useful from what lay between the covers of the books on the financial crisis table. I certainly didn't want to spend my dwindling resources buying any of them—not if I hoped to survive 'the two trillion-dollar meltdown,' and finish rich in 'a shattered economy.'

Lenny Writes

I got an e-mail from my cousin Lenny the other day. Hadn't heard from him for a long time. I'm always happy when, on those rare occasions, he calls or writes.

He started by saying "I hope this finds you and Janet well in these dizzying times." My wife is Janice, not Janet, but, as I said, it's been a long time.

"From what I've read," he continued, "rough fiscal shoals lie ahead."

"Uh oh," I thought, "this is not a good beginning."

He went on: "Many predict more big bank troubles, even failures; we even read of the likelihood of the collapse of the FDIC. While our money is in the Fort Knox Federal Credit Union (which won a 5-star rating recently), we're still nervous, not knowing if a large meltdown/collapse is in the cards."

It was 2012, and the financial crash was behind us. Lenny was worried about the next one and the safety of his funds. I wasn't aware that there was a Fort Knox Federal Credit Union, but if I were, I'd give it 5 stars for the name alone. And a "meltdown/collapse?" Sounds like he had seen the apocalypse, just a little late. Lenny is a professor whose field is medieval poetry. He's a little slow in picking up on current events and, I remembered, he did tend to worry a lot.

The e-mail continued: "Some predict rampant inflation and counsel buying real estate to protect one's savings; others see deflation coming and counsel buying government bonds. What is your own view of this plan?"

"What plan?" I asked myself.

I was, at the time, having some computer problems and it was only by chance that I got his message. I couldn't respond immediately. Two days later I got another e-mail, this time from Lennie's wife Louise. She thanked me in advance for the help I was about to give them.

Family! I began to compose a response. "The FDIC" I wrote, "is secure – a ward of the state that will be around as long as the government. The 'bail-outed' large banks," I added, "are unlikely to fail in the foreseeable future." And, I concluded, "the Fort Knox Federal Credit Union is probably okay. Even if it isn't, its shareholders are protected by the National Credit Union Administration in the same way that bank depositors are protected by the FDIC.

"Deflation," I told him, "is unlikely because the economy is still in recovery. Inflation," I added, "is more likely, especially if oil prices go through the roof. But short of political upheaval in the Middle East, price increases should be moderate until unemployment falls to low levels." As for "the plan," I told him that I couldn't comment without a lot more information than I had.

Looking over my response, I felt confident that it was squarely within the long tradition of economic ambiguity. It threw in a lot of 'likelies' and 'unlikelies,' and made no prediction that could turn out to be flat wrong. It gave no advice that could lead Lennie and his wife to claim I directed them over a cliff. My response was fully consistent with the guidance that frustrated Harry Truman enough to ask for a one-handed economist who couldn't tell him "on the one hand this, and on the other hand that." Its virtue was likely to be (there I go again) in its calming effect.

Lenny, Louise, and the whole world may be going to hell in a handbasket. Or not! But, after careful thought, I concluded there was no good answer to the questions that troubled their delayed awakening. With their eyes finally opened, they had joined the crisis-shocked crowd that will never again face their financial futures without morbid apprehension.

I hit "send."

That was weeks ago. I haven't heard from Lennie or Louise since. I don't expect to until, maybe, Krakatoa erupts again, or possibly a couple of years after.

It's Lenny Again

My cousin Lenny doesn't write often, but when he does, its usually because he worried about financial conditions. Back in 2012, it was the financial crisis of 2008. He wanted to know when the next one was coming. He also wanted to know whether the Fort Knox Credit Union, where he kept his funds, was safe. I told him I didn't think the next crisis was imminent, and that the Fort Knox Credit Union was probably as secure as, well, Fort Knox. My answers seemed to have a calming effect.

Lenny, as you might have guessed, doesn't normally keep abreast of financial conditions. He's a scholar whose primary field is medieval poetry. For him, current news is 'news on the Rialto' in 15th Century Venice. However, the pandemic had reignited his financial concerns. He had read that the Federal debt was about $27 trillion and rising; and that if you stacked a trillion one-dollar bills on top of one another, they would reach 67,866 miles into space.

"I'm worried," his message began. "When will the government go bankrupt; and what about the next-to-nothing interest rate the credit union is still paying. I might as well bury my money in the ground. And what does the Federal Reserve have to do with it?" Lenny had apparently learned something about the Federal Reserve since we last talked.

I like Lenny and I'm happy to hear from him, but I'm not happy about trying to answer the questions he asks. There are no easy answers for Lenny and it's a diversion from the book I'm writing, the one that's beginning to remind me of Gaudi's unfinished church in Barcelona that began construction 137 years ago. I might send him a reading list. But that would only produce new questions. On second thought, I won't respond at all. But then I would hear from Louise, his wife, who would want to know why I hadn't responded. Another question!

So I began to write. "Lenny, we are now in a recovery from the economic slide caused by the shut-downs intended to protect us from Covid19. The debt is rising because the government is borrowing to spend in the hope of helping people impacted by the shut-downs and to stimulate the economy. Interest rates are low because the Fed has ramped up the available supply of funds by buying all kinds of securities, federal government securities, municipal securities, mortgage-backed securities, and corporate bonds. It could buy oil drilling rigs to get them out of use to forestall global warming. Doesn't matter what it buys, its purchases create new funds that tend to lower interest rates.

"Right now the rate you're earning is close to zero because that's where the Federal Reserve wants it to be. Low rates raise the value of corporate stock and real estate, and encourage those who become wealthier to spend, and also to borrow and spend more. The Fed says it's going to keep rates low until, maybe, hell freezes over.

"The Fed doesn't care that your spending is limited by the rates the credit union pays. You might consider this an affront to your financial well-being. Some have thought Fed policy has been an affront to the nation's well-being, asserting that its policies have caused every financial crisis of the last 100 years; they have written books such as *The Creature from Jekyll Island* and *End the Fed*. But congress knows better. The Fed creates money, sometimes its policies work, and congress is always short of funds."

That, I decided, was enough. I left Lenny this time with the wisdom of Mr. Dooley, Peter Finley Dunne's bar-keep sage who dispensed memorable commentary on the affairs of the nation to his ever-present customer, Hennessy, a man who went to work each morning with a shovel on his shoulder. Hennessey had become agitated when banks began to close during the financial panic in 1907–as if he had money in a bank, which he didn't. Dooley told him: "All I say to ye Hinnissy is, be brave, be ca'm an' go on shovellin'."

I hit 'send!' I went back to my book muttering, "be brave, be calm...."

VII

MORTAL MEDITATION

One of the hardest things about growing older is seeing your relatives, friends and colleagues also grow older, develop illnesses and die. The first piece is about mortality, the second about a woman who I knew even longer that Janice and whose husband was a childhood friend and. then, there were others.

The Gift

A few years ago, my wife and children gave me several volumes of poetry by Mary Oliver that are a celebration of nature and of all living things. Somehow Mary Oliver got me thinking about a poem Carl Sandburg wrote in 1912 when he was 34 years old called "Limited." In the poem, he's riding on a train called the 'Limited Express, with 'fifteen steel coaches.' It's carrying 'a thousand people' and 'hurtling at high speed across the prairie.' He writes that the coaches will someday become "scrap and rust" and the people "will pass to ashes." He asks a man in the smoking car, where he's going. The man replies "Omaha."

~ ~ ~ ~

I read the poem when I was 19. Knowing everything worth knowing, I thought, how foolish these adults whose company I was about to join, pursuing their pursuits, unconscious of the hereafter, who couldn't tell 'Omaha' from "End-of-the-Line.'

Sixty years later, when I was pretty sure that the 'Limited

Express' had turned to 'scrap,' and Carl, himself, to ashes, I decided that the smoking-car man's, answer of "Omaha" was not foolish at all. He, no doubt, had things to do in Omaha. The poet, to point out the paradox, had things to do on the train, which for him involved the contemplation of ultimate extinction. They were both working at living in their own ways.

I saw Carl Sandburg, years ago, reading his poetry, playing guitar and singing the forgotten songs he had found in remote villages, mountain 'hollers' and river bottom encampments. I would have liked to talk to him about his experiences. But, I wondered, what would it have been to ride with him on the 'Limited' as he visualized oblivion. Somehow, I think, Mary Oliver would have been a better traveling companion.

I Remember Barbara

3:00 am
Noise fills the silent room
Oceans groan, Earth screeches
through its orbital plane, stars
boom in distant space

Barbara sits and waits.

I say hello
Her eyes lite-up
"I'm going home soon"
"What did you do today?"
She smiles
"I'm going home soon"

I ask if she remembered when we met, she
with Alan, years ago in a dim-lit coffee
house crowded tables, guitars, banjos
strumming through the coffee talk
I ask if she remembered when
sitting in her living room,
pole lamp, sofa, ottoman
kitchen floor, linoleum
talking into the night
babies on her knee
food and friends,
cars and work
waiting for
whatever
tomorrow
brings

"I'm going home soon"

Silence fills the silent room
Haunting smile, unlined face
muted thoughts of
time and place

Barbara remembers going home

The Death of Jim Marone

Thirty-five years ago, I watched Big Jim Marone lying in an open coffin at Saint Ann's. It was hard to believe. The other neighbors were also stunned. He was only 45 and, as far as we knew, never really sick.

Jim had a big job. He lived in Lawrenceville, just down the street, in a modern stone ranch house, on a one-acre wooded lot, with a wife and five children. The oldest was Cathy, about 14, who my wife hired, from time-to-time, as a baby-sitter. There were twin boys and two other girls.

Jim was the head of "Human Resources," née the Personnel Department, at a well-known international pharmaceutical company in New York City. He commuted to Manhattan, taking the 7:03am train from Princeton Junction every morning, arriving about an hour later at Penn Station. He returned every evening, usually on the 5:09, but sometimes later. The daily commute door-to-door was about 3 hours, but the trade-off was okay. His family lived in a pleasant, ex-urban area, outside the noise and dirt of the city. And they were better off financially than most in the neighborhood.

I worked with Jim when both of our sons were in the Cub Scouts. He had a lot of energy. But he was a dour and stand-offish man, some said arrogant. I didn't like him very much. He had strong opinions, and was rock-firm, almost menacing, when he had a point to make.

One day, our next-door neighbor who worked for the same pharmaceutical company, told me that Jim was in the hospital with a respiratory problem. A doctor who lived across the street had placed him there. Two days later Jim Marone was dead.

It was only then that it came out he had lost his job a year earlier and that he had never told his wife or family. He had just continued to commute to the city every day, as if nothing had changed. Without a salary, he had used his savings to meet his family's expenses.

I never learned why Jim didn't tell his wife what had happened, or how he spent what must have been long days in the city, sitting in an office that was still available, looking for another job. He never found one, at least one he would accept. He carried the burden alone during the last year of his life. When Jim died, he left his wife with five children to raise with a mortgage and no visible means of support. Their savings had been exhausted during his year of unemployment. The neighbors raised some money for them.

After all these years, death has become a grievously familiar–my mother, sister, father, aunts, uncles, cousins, colleagues and friends. But I still think about the death of Big Jim Marone. I'm not sure what went wrong. Whatever it was, I thought it said something about the morbidity of economic distress, the pathology of despair, and the dry rot of silence.

Lee Died

The picture Lee's wife sent showed him wearing a festive hat and a simple smile at what must have been an 80th birthday celebration. Fifty-five years ago, he had come from New York to the University of Wisconsin for graduate school. We shared an apartment in an old two-story house on the edge of campus with two others graduate students, one from South Africa and the other also from New York. Shortly after came the news he had Alzheimer's; soon he fell, fractured his spine and was in hospice. Then he died.

The apartment we shared had taken up most of one floor of the house and had two bedrooms, each with two beds. It was a broken-down survivor of nondescript architecture that should have been demolished a generation or two earlier. But it kept earning its keep by renting to students who had few alternatives.

We arose from our beds each morning to go to classes, to the library, to the student union on Lake Mendota, and to whatever other educational and social contacts we had with a wider circle of striving students in the same predicament. It was the womb out of which we climbed each day to meet the challenge and its uncertainties.

The year I roomed with Lee, I was employed as a research assistant by Ed Witte. I began to play the guitar with Jake and, as things turned out, made enduring friendships. It was a year in which the painful struggle of unending study and intense loneliness dissipated. I realized I would accomplish what I had set out to do. In the apartment that year, Lee was our peacemaker. He smoothed out the inevitable arguments, demonstrated remarkable equanimity and an unselfish interest in others. I did well enough that year to earn a fellowship the following year during which I wrote my dissertation.

When I left Wisconsin after earning my degree, I lost touch with Lee. But a mutual friend kept me informed of his comings and goings. I knew he had been teaching at a college in Wisconsin, was married and had retired in Madison

After nearly half-a-century absence, I was scheduled to return to

Madison for a conference. I contacted Lee and he invited me to his home for dinner. I was delighted to see him and meet his wife. I saw him again a few years later at a reunion on the University campus.

On hearing of his death, I thought about his career. It wasn't particularly notable. The Ph.D. was, among other things, a license to teach in college, and he did that. But it was also a research degree and, as far as I knew, he had never undertaken any research or engaged in the traditional pursuit of publication. He retired early for a professor, at about the age of 63. He had, however, a life outside the career for which we had trained, and he found interests beyond his profession. When I saw him after nearly a half-century, he seemed the same, easy-going and comfortable.

Lee and many others with whom I had professional or personal relationships are now gone. I wonder at the accumulation of experience, knowledge, joy, concern and sorrow that was extinguished with their passing. How is this possible? Doesn't it violate some universal physical law, perhaps the one about the conservation of energy? I know, I know that this is just another way of asking the same old unanswerable question.

I remember Lee's even-temper and abundance of good will. I remember walking with him on State Street, between the University campus and the state capitol, talking about the merits of pecan waffles and bratwurst, and marveling at Ella Fitzgerald who made an appearance at a jazz club near us. I have begun to understand that, in the end, all that remains of all that energy are memories.

Shining Cover

Another day passed away, gone without consent
dark mystery of hopes and whispers of despair,
bright sun rising, giving light and warmth
shining cover of an unread book

Ira

(Read at his memorial service, July 2016)

I had an aunt, now dead–a very religious person. She once told me that it was necessary at a memorial service to speak about the departed to speed their departure to wherever they were bound.

~ ~ ~ ~

Ira has been in my mind since his birth. I still picture him in the hospital when, after his mother labored for 22 hours, he finally decided to join us. I see him at four years old, laughing while riding his tricycle through puddles of water to greet me as I arrived home from work; and I see him at ten or eleven, diving to catch a baseball I had lifted into the air in our backyard. I hear him in his 30s, speaking eloquently at his grandfathers' funeral when I was too shocked to speak. I see him and hear him in hundreds of other comings and goings, talking about music, movies, sports, his work and mine, occasionally politics, economics, even the Federal Reserve, and in other fragments of our lives over his shortened 52 years of living.

He was, throughout his life, filled with child-like wonder at the world around him. He read stories and then he made up stories, wonderful tales of mystery and adventure. From the time he was first able to write, what he wrote was magical. He had the gift to move people, to make them laugh and to make them cry. In his writing and in other ways, he revealed the generous nature of his inner-self; and an internal strength that helped him over the inevitable rough times.

Ira had a firm grasp on what he wanted to do and what he did not want to do. He wanted to exert his talents through work, but he also wanted to be with his wife, his family and his friends. He pursued friendships, and that brought him happiness.

I can never forget that he was here–and with deep, wordless sorrow that he is no longer here. In his last two years of struggle,

85

through operations, physical pain and mental anguish riddled by the knowledge of the likely outcome, he told us how he approached what was to come. It was the approach the Roman poet Virgil put to words 2000 years ago when he said: "Death plucks my ear and says, Live–I am coming."

~ ~ ~ ~

I speak these thoughts in the fervent hope that my aunt knew what she was talking about, and that what I have said helps speed my son to wherever it is that the best of us, and the ones we cherish beyond conscious understanding, go when they are gone.

Pelican on the Library Steps

I give it wide berth
maneuvering to observe from the front
a large pelican standing statue-still
on the stepping-stone path
to the library door

The unblinking vision catches light,
cast its shadow on cloistered archives
row on row of what is known
in layered shelves beyond the wall
projecting what's not known at all

Where did the pelican come from?
How did it get here
and why?

The sun bright, I close my eyes,
begin to rise above the land
sounds grow distant, muted now
below, off-white sand,
people, blankets, chairs
the beach revealed:
repeating ovals of umbrella tops
like turtle shells, hiding those
sitting on weathered grains of
granulated rock

Those under the umbrella shells,
separated from the amniotic fluid,
from which they came, approach
with caution an ancestral home
that awaken fearful memories

The sun sends streaks of light
across the water uncovering in reflection
morsels for birds that parade and dance
along a twisting, turning band
that marks the start and end of land

On the library steps
the pelican sleeps with one eye open,
dreaming, soaring, plunging,
a presentiment

A flap of wings, the bird rises,
circles westward toward the Gulf,
portending something lost,
something of immeasurable worth
drifting between land and sea
hovering in my memory

VIII

A THERAPEUTIC DISTRACTION

Songs of the Sea

...a sail drew nearer and nearer, and picked me up at last. It was the devious-cruising Rachel, that in her retracing search after her missing children, only found another orphan.

Ishmael, *Moby Dick*

Of all the stories, short and long, I've ever heard and read
Of fairy queens and warrior kings, the living and the dead
Of soldiers, sailors and marines, of cars and trains and air
machines
Of cowboys, tramps and engineers, of unknown lands and pioneers
Those that most appeal to me are wooden ships and men at sea

The wooden ships at anchor somewhere across the bar,
The men who sailed for Rio below the southern star

Those who climbed the mizzen mast, anchors they did weigh
Who rounded the stormy Cape of Horn for Valparaiso Bay

Those who sailed many a league, let davit tackles fall
Who looked for land, hunted whales, and fit the rigging tall

The men who spotted mermaids, that told to their dismay
Of three times round their ship went down to perish in the sea

Cape cod girls, neat they were, without the help of combs,
Combed their hair, the legend goes, with oily cod fish bones

Sailors who bid those Spanish girls, a smiling, sad adieu
Returning to New Bedford town, captain, mates and crew

Seaman buried in the sea with widows left to weep
Service of the silent dead and storms their vigil keep

And then there was Columbus, waking just once more
To imagine in the distance the unimagined shore

Of all the stories, short and long, I've ever heard and read
Of fairy queens and warrior kings, the living and the dead
These are the ones that stir my soul, and ramble through my
thoughts
Sea songs, after all these years, stories of the sea
They roll in waves across my mind, and Ishmael calls to me.

IX

AGING

Reflections on Getting Older

He had the firm features and bald head of the mature Yule Brenner in "The King and I", and the body of Arnold Schwarzenegger in "The Terminator". He smiled out at me from the Sunday paper, "one hundred and sixty-four pounds of lean muscle tissue" and "10% body fat". The message continued: "How can this 68-year-old medical doctor have the body of a 30-Year-Old?" The answer: "Cenegenics" – a revolutionary approach to aging that reduces the risk of disease, improves muscle tone, increases energy and libido; sharpens thinking and, in general, improves one's disposition. There followed a website on which to register, and a phone number to call. On calling, it promised a connection to a clinical professor at a well-known medical school who would answer all questions. It also promised the call would be "strictly confidential."

I am normally skeptical about outrageous advertising claims, and recognize the possibility of photoshopping the heads of older men on the bodies of young bodybuilders, but Cenegenics got me thinking. T.S. Eliot recognized aging in 'wearing the bottoms of my trousers rolled.' I recognize aging by remembering that I saw T.S. Eliot read his poetry. I have lived long enough to see copying machines and scanners replace carbon paper, and Dick Tracy's wrist-watch phone emerge in Apple advertisements. I saw Ted Williams play against the Philadelphia Athletics the year he batted 407, and my trousers are getting long.

Most everyone makes an effort to 'live long and prosper,' and to stay young in the process. The effort is intensified by a cultural disparagement of the elderly in popular sayings, stories and song: "There's no fool like an old fool;" "You can't teach an old dog new tricks;" Dorian Gray went so far as to made a pact with the devil to keep a youthful appearance, while a picture showed him crumbling as he aged. The Beatles serenaded us "Will you still need me, will you still feed me when I'm 64."

Nothing wrong with making the effort to stay young. There is something wrong with giving up too early. Mickey Mantle, after a life of hard living, famously said "If I had known I was going to live this long, I'd have taken better care of myself!" He died at the age of 63, not realizing that the early deaths of his father, grandfather and other relatives was not a family trait but due to their inhaling zinc and lead dust from working in the mines.

Mickey never expected old age; others have looked forward to it. Hokusai, the great Japanese painter rose from poverty, taught himself to draw and kept drawing Mount Fuji, at least 36 views. When he was 75, he said:

"From the age of six I had a mania for drawing....but all I have produced before the age of seventy is not worth taking into account...." By the time "I am 110, everything I do, be it but a dot or a line, will be alive. I beg those who live as long as I to see if I do not keep my word."

Hokusai died when he was 89, still striving, I like to think, to get Mount Fuji right.

So, I come full circle with these ruminations on the age-old issue of aging. I don't know about the 68-year-old doctor with the body of Arnold Schwarzenegger, but I think I'll pass on Cenegenics. Hokusai probably had the right idea, even though he didn't make it to 110. And he probably got Mount Fuji right the first time.

Beats

Have you ever *watched* your heart beat?
I don't mean heard it or felt it,
I mean have you actually ever watched it?
I have

Or at least a fuzzy image on a monitor
collecting blood and pumping it into an artery
green and blue splashes of light appearing,
disappearing

I watched and thought about my heart
grinding away, air whooshing through my lungs
gas gurgling, joints clacking, nerves
humming

Thumping, blowing, whistling wails
a cacophony of rhythms and tones
a ringing, jingling, banging, clanging, traveling
one-man band

Making music never heard,
persistent and unbound
an echoed hymn of life and limb
silent sound

Vibrations entwine with Mozart, Bach
Prokofiev, Gershwin, Dylan and Scruggs
and the remarkable others who come gig bag
in hand

With strings, horns keyboard and voice
to join in melodic communion with the
green and blue splashes of light in the
chambers of our hearts

My Musical Life

When I was very young, 3 or 4, I remember hearing my mother singing: "A capital ship on an ocean trip was the Walloping Window Blind. No wind that blew dismayed her crew or troubled the captain's mind." I learned later that the song had a line with a hidden, off-color, meaning. She would have been mortified.

Much later, when I was about 10 or 11, my parents decided that I should learn to play an instrument. They told me I had a distant cousin who played violin in the Philadelphia Orchestra. My grandmother had sent her son, my uncle, to him for lessons when he was about my age. After one session, my cousin sent him back with the advice that she hide the violin and never send him back again.

That did not dissuade them from having me learn to play something. My parents interviewed a few teachers peddling lessons on various instruments. The one I liked was an Hawaiian guitarist. He slid a steel bar across the strings, emitting the whining sound of 'Aloha.' But I think the sound irritated my parents. I ended up with an old upright piano and a teacher who, to my eyes, was ancient. She was pencil thin with long hair and a wrinkled disposition. I believe she taught 3rd grade at the elementary school.

I took lessons for about 6 months. I learned the basics of reading music and could play "American Patrol," and a little bit of "Summertime" I thought it was okay. But I preferred being outside playing ball with the other kids on the block, and soon tired of practice. I was sprung by my parents who, I believe, were not truly devoted to the music I was playing.

My next memory of musical exposure came when I was about 16. I found an Ella Fitzgerald record with a Gershwin song that began, "I was doing all right...'til you came by." Having entered into a troublesome relationship with a young lady, I could relate. I played it repeatedly until the grooves wore out and the young lady disappeared.

My musical life then went into hiatus. I turned, instead, to the rhythm of basketball and the dissonance of writing for the school newspaper. It wasn't until my sophomore year in college that I met another girl, a charismatic adventurer who was deep into folk culture, the Spanish Civil War, Diego Rivera and the Mexican revolution. She knew songs like "Los Cuatro Generales." I bought a ukulele and began to strum a few chords.

In my final two years in college, two musical events made a lasting impression. On a warm summer night, I sat with a friend on a grassy hill at Robin Hood Dell, an outdoor concert venue in Fairmount Park. We listened to Yehudi Menuhin whose violin, I decided, emitted the most beautiful sounds I had ever heard. The next year, I attended a performance by Paul Robeson at a run-down concert hall in center city Philadelphia. He sang spirituals accompanied by his pianist, Lawrence Brown. I was amazed at Robeson's precise control of each note as it emerged *basso profundo* from somewhere deep within his body.

By now I had mastered the ukulele–I could imitate Arthur Godfrey playing "In the Blue Ridge Mountains of Virginia." I decided to expand my horizons and bought an inexpensive guitar. I had no idea how to play it. But I took it with me to graduate school, first to Illinois and then to Wisconsin. In Wisconsin I met Jake, the biophysicist whose preferred instrument was the banjo. But he was also good on the guitar. It turned out, I had a decent ear, flexible fingers and a memory that permitted me to pick out melodies.

When I completed my graduate education and moved East, I laid my guitar to rest in a closet where it resided for the better part of fifty years, replaced by the urgency to succeed as an economist and a teacher. On my retirement from teaching, I found reasons to pick up my guitar again. I begin to play with Chris, a woman who had been cleaning our house for decades and who had become a friend. In her youth, she had played the guitar and sang with her parents at bars and restaurants in the Lambertville-New Hope area. I joined the Princeton Folk Music Society and found kindred souls who had been playing various folk instruments since Pete Seeger was a pup.

Today I listen to Beethoven in Richardson Hall on the Princeton campus, and to Chris Thile play Bach on the mandolin, along with his interpretation of an Appalachian picker's delight, "There's a rabbit in the log, and I ain't got no dog...." Simple or complex, I'm convinced that we all march to the beat of some song we inhaled in our childhood, like that shady but irrepressible "capital ship on an ocean trip." I would have liked to have played the Hawaiian guitar that my parents dismissed; and also, after hearing Yehudi Menuhin, to have made an attempt at the violin. I would like to have taken lessons from my dyspeptic cousin with the Philadelphia Orchestra. I can only imagine what he would have said.

Tomes

The books sit silent on the shelves, each
in its assigned space, scholarly works
texts, treatises, articles assembled
biography, autobiography rub
shoulders with old reports
and government
publications

waiting like Chinese stone soldiers,
terra cotta army of Qin Shi Huang
paper and cloth fighting men
armed with the accumulated
learning of ages waiting to
be buried for protection
in the afterlife

some shout jackets, brightly colored
shamelessly appealing, seductive
others whisper, covers gone
marked by age, pages torn
binding ripped, damaged
spine, margin notes
underlined

magical ideas of time and place
a library of words enshrined
within the marvels of an
earlier age, spanning
fabled urgencies a
strange design
for comity

each had come forward, a parading gift
now the lumbering army sits
encamped on wood worn
shelves, cloth and paper
soldiers, lost in time,
waiting for the
afterlife

X

A WHISPERED AFTERTHOUGHTS

Birthday at Spring Lake in Early June

The scattered clouds occasionally block out the sun, evoking a sense of twilight at one o'clock in the afternoon.

Sitting on a bench, I watch walkers on the boardwalk, and the occasional runner breathing heavily, pounding past.

Beyond the boardwalk, the pristine beach, almost empty, rock jetties bracketing the waves relentlessly breaking on light sand

In the distance, the gray sky descends to meet the gray ocean, two slabs converging, leaving a living space within the angle of intersection.

So it went on a memorable birthday at a prosperous Jersey beach town where Sammy 'the Bull' Gravano was reputed to have once owned a home, and where bootlegger Bill McCoy, 'the real McCoy,' landed kegs of rum from fast ships during prohibition

I lay back on a bench dedicated to "the Rizzo brothers, David, Mike and Joe, whose feet may wander, but whose memories are here" with all who sit and ponder

the sand running down to the sea, and the day they arrived.

ABOUT THE AUTHOR

Bernard Shull is an economist, author of articles and books on money, banking, financial markets and the Federal Reserve. He lives with his wife Janice in Lawrenceville, New Jersey, and sometimes in Naples, Florida where he plunged into the cheerful and challenging world of expressive writing

Made in the USA
Middletown, DE
07 December 2022

16200639R10066